Mountain Biking
Bend

SCOTT RAPP

FALCON® Helena, Montana

A FALCON GUIDE ®

Falcon® Publishing is continually expanding its list of recreational guide-books. All books include detailed descriptions, accurate maps, and all the information necessary for enjoyable trips. You can order extra copies of this book and get information and prices for other Falcon guidebooks by writing Falcon, P.O. Box 1718, Helena, MT 59624 or calling toll free 1-800-582-2665. Also, please ask for a free copy of our current catalog. Visit our website at http:\\www.falconguide.com

©1998 by Falcon® Publishing Inc., Helena, Montana

2 3 4 5 6 7 8 9 10 TP 03 02 01 00 99 98

Falcon and FalconGuide are registered trademarks of Falcon® Publishing Inc.

Printed in Canada.

Cover photo by Mike Houska/Borland Stock Photo.

Library of Congress Cataloging-in-Publication Data

Rapp, Scott, 1969–
    Mountain biking Bend / by Scott Rapp.
        p. cm.
    ISBN 1-56044-593-9 (pbk. paper)
    1. All terrain cycling–Oregon–Bend–Guidebooks. 2. Trails—Oregon—Bend—Guidebooks. 3. Bend (Or.)—Guidebooks. I. Title.
GV1045.5.072B467   1998   97-50137
                                                        CIP

CAUTION
Outdoor recreational activities are by their very nature potentially hazardous. All participants in such activities must assume the responsibility for their own actions and safety. The information contained in this guidebook cannot replace sound judgment and good decision-making skills, which help reduce the risk exposure, nor does the scope of this book allow for disclosure of all the potential hazards and risks involved in such activities.

    Learn as much as possible about the outdoor recreational activities in which you participate, prepare for the unexpected, and be cautious. The reward will be a safer and more enjoyable experience.

♻ Text pages printed on recycled paper.

Contents

Acknowledgments

A lot of solo riding went into the production of this book, but I was rarely alone in my effort—thanks to the support of my friends and family.

To Amy for putting up with my not always cheerful mood during production and accompanying me on countless research rides.

Fixing broken wheels is not one of my limited talents, so thanks to the gang at Hutch's Bicycles for not tiring of my frequent visits.

To the helpful staff at the Deschutes National Forest offices, including Marv Lang, Bernadine Murphy, and Steve Hayden, for taking my frequent calls, answering questions, and proofing ride descriptions.

To the crews at many local bike shops, such as Sunnyside Sports, Century Cycles, Chrome Pony, Summit Sports, and Eurosports, for sharing information and always having just what I needed.

To my parents for kicking me in the butt whenever I needed it.

And finally to Henry dog for encouraging frequent breaks from the computer or drawing table.

MAP LEGEND

 Trail

 Unimproved Road

 Paved Road

 Gravel Road

 Interstate

 Wilderness Boundary

Waterway

Lake/Reservoir

Δ Λ Camping/Shelter

City or Metropolitan Area

(37) Trailhead

X Elevation

(15) Interstate

(12) U.S. Highway

(200) State Highway

88 Forest or County Road

●━━● Gate

) (Pass

 Ski Area

N
↑ Compass

0 1
███ Scale
MILES

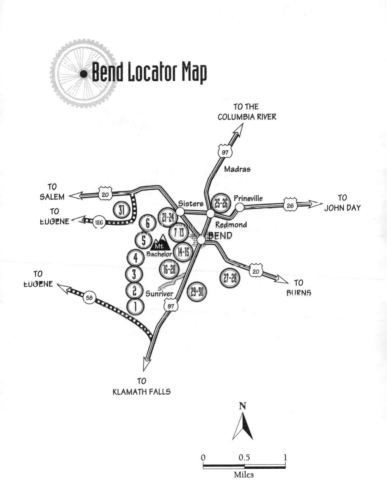

Bend Locator Map

TO THE
COLUMBIA RIVER

97

Madras

TO
SALEM

20

TO
EUGENE

126

31

Sisters

25-26

Prineville

26

TO
JOHN DAY

21-24

Redmond

6

7 13

BEND

5

Mt.
Bachelor

14-15

4

16-20

3

27-28

20

TO
BURNS

2

29-30

TO
EUGENE

58

1

Sunriver

97

TO
KLAMATH FALLS

N

0   0.5   1
Miles

Get Ready to CRANK!

Where to ride? It's a quandary that faces every mountain biker, beginner or expert, local or expatriate.

If you're new to the area, where do you start? If you're a long-time local, how do you avoid the rut of riding the same old trails week after week? And how do you find new terrain that's challenging but not overwhelming? Or pick an easier ride for when your not-so-serious buddies want to come along?

Welcome to *Mountain Biking Bend*. Here are 31 rides ranging from easy road routes to smooth singletrack to bravado-busting boulder fields. The rides are described in plain language, with accurate distances and ratings for physical and technical difficulty. Each entry offers a wealth of detailed information that's easy to read and use, from an armchair or on the trail.

Our aim here is threefold: to help you choose a ride that's appropriate for your fitness and skill level; to make it easy to find the trailhead; and to help you complete the ride safely, without getting lost. Take care of these basics and fun is bound to break loose.

Bend's Backcountry:
What to Expect

The rides in this book cover a wide variety of terrain. Most of the rides are mountainous, exposed, or both and that means two things: they can be steep and rough, and inclement weather is always a threat.

Mountain terrain requires preparedness. Get in good shape before you attempt any of these rides, and know your limits. Keep your bike running smoothly with frequent cleaning and maintenance. Do a quick check before each ride to ensure that tires, rims, brakes, handlebars, seat, shifters, derailleurs, and chain all survived the last ride intact and are functioning properly.

Always carry at least one water bottle, though two are recommended (don't forget to fill them). Snacks, such as fruit or sports energy bars, will help keep those mighty thighs cranking for many hours. Dress for the weather and pack a wind- and water-proof jacket whenever there's any doubt about a clear sky. Don't forget sunglasses, sunscreen, lip balm, and insect repellent, as needed.

I tend to go light on tools, with a pump, spare tube, a small multi-tool, and some duct tape. This extra pound of gear could make the difference between arriving home a few minutes late and spending the night out on the trail. Some folks aren't comfortable unless they bring 20 pounds of tools; you can usually hear them jangling up the trail, but they rarely get stranded by mechanical problems.

This book is designed to be easily carried along in a jersey pocket or bike bag, and the maps and ride descriptions will help anyone unfamiliar with the trails. A more detailed book is available from the same author. It's called *Mountain Biking Central Oregon*, and features topographical maps with brief descriptions of each ride.

Cycling gloves are also essential safety equipment, saving hands from cuts and bruises from falls and encroaching branches and rocks. They also improve your grip and comfort on the handlebars. Finally, always wear a helmet; it can save your life.

Bend's **weather** spans the gamut of North American extremes, particularly in the surrounding mountains. Snow can fall any day of the year, but summer highs may top 100 degrees Fahrenheit. In general, higher elevations are cooler (by as much as 10 degrees for every 1,000 feet gained) and windier. If you are driving to a trailhead, play it safe and take a variety of clothes in the car to match the variable weather you may encounter.

Bend is remarkable among mountain bike towns in that many local rides are open year-round. In February, while skiers may be enjoying a 200-inch snow base 20 miles west of town, mountain bikers are cruising beautiful desert rides 20 miles east of town. In fact, many of the desert rides are better during the winter months because the tread remains firm. The soil in the high desert is actually better for riding after both light and heavy rains. Mud is almost nonexistent in central Oregon and appears only during the spring thaw when the frozen ground does not let melting snow soak in. Local riders often spend August and September wishing for rains to come and pack down the dust.

The yearly number of rainy or snowy days tends to increase the closer you go to the Cascade Range. While snow or rain may be falling at Swampy Lakes, the sun is usually shining brightly at Smith Rock. The high Cascades form a barrier to incoming storms, resulting in a very noticeable rain shadow. In general, expect lots of sunshine.

Trails to the east of Bend are best ridden in the fall, winter, and spring (except after heavy snowfalls). The exception to this rule is Pine Mountain, which at 6,500 feet is high enough to maintain a significant snowpack during winter and early spring. The farther west you go from town into the Cascade Range, the deeper the snowpack will be. While Phil's Trail may open to biking by April, Forest Road 370 is rarely open before mid-July. Ask at a USDA Forest Service office or local bike shop for up-to-date information.

Compared to riding the west side of the Cascades, most of the routes in Central Oregon are fairly gentle. Many of the rides in this book have gradual climbs and are not overly technical. There are several notable exceptions, but as a rule expect lots of cruising terrain with occasional challenges thrown in.

Rules of the Trail

If every mountain biker always yielded the right-of-way, stayed on the trail, avoided wet or muddy trails, never cut switchbacks, never skidded, always rode in control, showed respect for other trail users, and carried out every last scrap of what was carried in (candy wrappers and bike-part debris included)—in short, *did the right thing*—then we wouldn't need a list of rules governing our behavior.

Fact is, most mountain bikers are conscientious and are trying to do the right thing. Most of us *own* that integrity. (No one becomes good at something as demanding and painful as grunting up sheer mountainsides by cheating.)

Most of us don't need rules. But we do need knowledge. What exactly is the right thing to do?

Here are some guidelines—I like to think of them as reminders—reprinted by permission from the International Mountain Bicycling Association (IMBA). The basic theme here is to reduce or eliminate any damage to the land and water, the plant and wildlife inhabitants, and other backcountry visitors and trail users. Ride with respect.

IMBA Rules of the Trail

Thousands of miles of dirt trails have been closed to mountain bikers, including some in central Oregon. The irresponsible riding habits of a few riders have been a factor. Do your part to maintain trail access by observing the following rules of the trail, formulated by the International Mountain Bicycling Association (IMBA). IMBA's mission is to promote environmentally sound and socially responsible mountain biking.

1. Ride on open trails only. Respect trail and road closures (ask if not sure), avoid possible trespass on private land, and obtain permits and authorization as may be required. Federal and state wilderness areas are closed to cycling. The way you ride will influence trail management decisions and policies.

2. Leave no trace. Be sensitive to the dirt beneath you. Even on open (legal) trails, you should not ride under conditions where you will leave evidence of your passing, such as on certain soils after a rain. Recognize different types of soil and trail construction; practice low-impact cycling. This also means staying on existing trails and not creating any new ones. Be sure to pack out at least as much as you pack in.

3. Control your bicycle! Inattention for even a second can cause problems. Obey all bicycle speed regulations and recommendations.

4. Always yield trail. Make known your approach well in advance. A friendly greeting (or bell) is considerate and works well; don't startle others. Show your respect when passing by slowing to a walking pace or even stopping. Anticipate other trail users around corners or in blind spots.

5. Never spook animals. All animals are startled by an unannounced approach, a sudden movement, or a loud noise. This can be dangerous for you, others, and the animals. Give animals extra room and time to adjust to you. When passing horses use special care and follow directions from the horseback riders (ask if uncertain). Running cattle and disturbing wildlife is a serious offense. Leave gates as you found them, or as marked.

6. Plan ahead. Know your equipment, your ability, and the area in which you are riding—and prepare accordingly. Be self-sufficient at all times, keep your equipment in good repair, and carry necessary supplies for changes in weather or other conditions. A well-executed trip is a satisfaction to you and not a burden or offense to others. Always wear a helmet.

Keep trails open by setting a good example of environmentally sound and socially responsible off-road cycling.

How to Use this Guide

Mountain Biking Bend describes 31 mountain bike rides in their entirety. Five other local routes are described with less detail in Appendix A.

Many of the featured rides are loops, beginning and ending at the same point but coming and going on different trails. Loops are by far the most popular type of ride, and Bendites are lucky to have so many so close to home.

Be forewarned, however: the difficulty of a loop ride may change dramatically depending on which direction you ride around the loop. If you are unfamiliar with the rides in this book, try them first as described here. The directions follow the path of least resistance (which does not necessarily mean "easy"). After you've been over the terrain, you can determine whether a given loop would be fun—or even feasible—in the reverse direction.

Portions of some rides follow gravel and even paved roads, and a handful of rides never wander off road. Purists may wince at road rides in a book about mountain biking, but these are special rides. They offer a chance to enjoy mountain scenery and fresh air while covering easier, non-technical terrain for people new to the sport. They can also be used by hard-core riders on "active rest" days or when higher elevation trails are closed by mud or snow.

Each ride description in this book follows the same format:

Number and Name of the Ride: Rides are cross-referenced by number throughout this book. In many cases, parts of rides or entire routes can be linked to other rides for longer trips or variations on a standard route. These opportunities are noted, followed by "see Ride(s) #."

For the names of rides I relied on official names of trails, roads, and natural features as shown on national forest and U.S. Geological Survey maps. Several of the trails in this guide are new and do not appear on these maps.

Location: The general whereabouts of the ride; distance and direction from Bend.

Distance: The length of the ride in miles, given as a loop, one way, or round-trip.

Time: An estimate of how long it takes to complete the ride; for example, 1 to 2 hours. *The time listed is the actual riding time and does not include rest stops.* Strong, skilled riders may be able to do a given ride in less than the estimated time, while other riders may take considerably longer. Also bear in mind that severe weather, changes in trail conditions, or mechanical problems may prolong a ride.

Elevation gain: This is the total elevation gain as recorded by an altimeter. These figures are estimates but will give you a feel for how much climbing a given ride requires.

Tread: The type of road or trail: paved road, gravel road, dirt road or jeep track, doubletrack, ATV-width singletrack, and singletrack.

Season: The seasons best suited for riding, taking into account precipitation and trail conditions.

Aerobic level: The level of physical effort required to complete the ride: easy, moderate, or strenuous. (See the explanation of the rating systems on page [ ]).

Technical difficulty: The level of bike handling skills needed to complete the ride upright and in one piece. Technical difficulty is rated on a scale from 1 to 5, with 1 being the easiest (see the explanation of the rating systems on page [ ]).

Hazards: A list of dangers that may be encountered on a ride, including traffic, weather, trail obstacles and conditions, risky stream crossings, difficult route-finding, and other perils. Remember: conditions may change at any time. Be alert for storms, new fences, downfall, missing trail signs, and mechanical failure. Fatigue, heat, cold, and/or dehydration may impair judgment. Always wear a helmet and other safety equipment. Ride in control at all times.

Highlights: Special features or qualities that make a ride worth doing (as if we needed an excuse!): scenery, fun singletrack, access to other routes, chances to see wildlife.

Land status: A list of managing agencies or land owners. Most of the rides in this book are on the Deschutes National Forest or lands administered by the Bureau of Land Management. But many of the rides also cross portions of private, state, or municipal lands. Always leave gates as you found them. And respect the land, regardless of who owns it. See Appendix B for a list of local addresses for land-managing agencies.

Maps: A list of available maps. The Deschutes National Forest map is a good overview resource for those rides within its boundaries, though many of the rides in this guide are administered by other agencies. The map in *Mountain Biking Central Oregon* is an excellent resource, providing a good overall look at most of these rides, along with text and elevation contours, all on waterproof paper.

Access: How to find the trailhead or the start of the ride. A number of rides can be pedaled right from town; for others, it's best to drive to the trailhead.

The ride: A mile-by-mile list of key points—landmarks, notable climbs and descents, stream crossings, obstacles, hazards, major turns and junctions—along the ride. All distances were measured to the tenth of a mile with a cyclo-computer (a bike-mounted odometer). Terrain, riding technique, and even tire pressure can affect odometer readings, so treat all mileages as estimates.

Finally, one last reminder that the real world is changing all the time: the information presented here is as accurate and up-to-date as possible, but there are no guarantees out in the mountains. You alone are responsible for your safety and for the choices you make on the trail. If you do find an error or omission in this book, or a new and noteworthy change in the field, I'd like to hear from you. Please write to Scott Rapp, c/o Falcon Publishing, P.O. Box 1718, Helena, MT 59624.

Elevation Graphs

An elevation profile accompanies each ride description to help you determine how easy or hard the ride is. Also weigh other factors such as elevation above sea level, total trip distance, weather and wind, and current trail conditions.

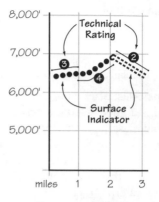

Rating the Rides—One Person's Pain is Another's Pleasure

One of the first lessons learned by most mountain bikers is to not trust their friends' accounts of how easy or difficult a given ride may be.

"Where ya wanna' ride today?"

"Let's do 'The Wall,' dudes—it's gnarly in the middle, but even my grandma could fly up that last hill, and the view is way cool."

If you don't read between the lines, only painful experience will tell you that granny won the pro-elite class in last weekend's hillclimb race, and "the view" is over the handlebars from the lip of a thousand-foot drop on that fun little gnarly stretch.

So how do you know what you're getting into, before it's too late?

Don't always listen to your friends. But do read this book. Falcon guides rate each ride for two types of difficulty: the *physical effort* required to pedal the distance, and the level of *bike-handling skills* needed to stay upright and make it home in one piece. We call these **Aerobic level** and **Technical difficulty.**

The following sections explain what the various ratings mean in plain, specific language.

Aerobic Level Ratings

Bicycling is often touted as a relaxing, low-impact, relatively easy way to burn excess calories and maintain a healthy heart and lungs. Mountain biking, however, tends to pack a little more work (and excitement) into the routine.

Fat tires and soft or rough trails increase the rolling resistance, so it takes more effort to push those wheels around. And unpaved or off-road hills tend to be steeper than grades measured and tarred by the highway department. When we use the word *steep*, we mean a sweat-inducing, oxygen-sucking, lactose-building climb. If it's followed by an exclamation point—steep (!)—expect some honest pain on the way up (and maybe for days afterward).

So expect to breathe hard and sweat some, probably a lot. Pedaling around town is a good start, but it won't fully prepare you for the workout offered by most of the rides in this book. If you're unsure of your level of fitness, see a doctor for a physical exam before tackling any of these rides. And if you're riding to get back in shape, or just for the fun of it, take it easy. Walk or rest if need be. Start with short rides and add miles gradually.

Here's how we rate the exertion level for terrain covered in this book:

Easy: Flat or gently rolling terrain. No steeps or prolonged climbs.

Moderate: Some hills. Climbs may be short and fairly steep or

11

long and gradual.

Strenuous: Frequent or prolonged climbs steep enough to require riding in the lowest gear; requires a high level of aerobic fitness, power, and endurance (typically acquired through many hours of riding and proper training). Less fit riders may need to walk.

Many rides are mostly easy and moderate but may have short strenuous sections. Other rides are mostly strenuous and should be attempted only after a complete medical checkup and implant of a second heart, preferably a *big* one. Also be aware that flailing through a highly technical section can be exhausting even on the flats. Good riding skills and a relaxed stance on the bike save energy.

Finally, any ride can be strenuous if you ride it hard and fast. Conversely, the pain of a lung-burning climb grows easier to tolerate as your fitness level improves. Learn to pace yourself and remember to schedule easy rides and rest days into your calendar.

Technical Difficulty Ratings

While you're pushing up that steep, strenuous slope, wondering how much farther you can go before your lungs prolapse and billow out of your mouth like an air bag in a desperate gasp for oxygen, remember that the dry heaves aren't the only hurdle on the way to the top of the mountain. There's that tree across the trail, or the sideslope full of ball bearing–sized pebbles, or the place where the trail disappears except for faint bits of rubber clinging to the sheer wall of lava straight ahead.

Mountain bikes will roll over or through an amazing array of life's little challenges, but sometimes we, as riders, have to help—or at least close our eyes and hang on. As a last resort, some riders get off their bikes and walk (get this) *before* they flip over the handlebars. These folks have no sense of adventure. The rest of us hop onto our bikes with only the dimmest inkling of what lies ahead, and later brag about the ride to hell (leaving out the part about carrying our bikes half the distance because hell has some highly technical terrain).

No more. The technical difficulty ratings in this book help take the worst surprises out of backcountry rides. In the privacy of your own home you can make an honest appraisal of your bike-handling skills and then find rides in these pages that are within your ability.

We rate technical difficulty on a scale from 1 to 5, from easiest to most difficult. We tried to make the ratings as objective as possible by considering the type of obstacles and their frequency of occurrence. The same standards were applied consistently through all the rides in this book.

We've also added plus (+) and minus (-) symbols to cover gray areas between given levels of difficulty: a 4+ obstacle is harder than a 4, but easier than a -5. A stretch of trail rated as 5+ would be unrideable by all but the most skilled (or luckiest) riders.

Here are the five levels defined:

Level 1: Smooth tread; road or doubletrack; no obstacles, ruts, or steeps. Requires basic bike-riding skills.

Level 2: Mostly smooth tread; wide, well-groomed singletrack or road/doubletrack with minor ruts or loose gravel or sand.

Level 3: Irregular tread with some rough sections; single or doubletrack with obvious route choices; some steep sections. Occasional obstacles may include small rocks, roots, waterbars, ruts, loose gravel or sand, and sharp turns or broad, open switchbacks.

Level 4: Rough tread with few smooth places; singletrack or rough doubletrack with limited route choices; steep sections, some with obstacles. Obstacles are numerous and varied, including rocks, roots, branches, ruts, sidehills, narrow tread, loose gravel or sand, and switchbacks.

Level 5: Continuously broken, rocky, root-infested, or trenched tread; singletrack or extremely rough doubletrack with few route choices; frequent, sudden, and severe changes in gradient; some slopes so steep that wheels lift off ground. Obstacles are nearly continuous and may include boulders, logs, water, large holes, deep ruts, ledges, piles of loose gravel, steep sidehills, encroaching trees, and tight switchbacks.

Again, most of the rides in this book cover varied terrain, with an ever-changing degree of technical difficulty. Some trails run smooth with only occasional obstacles, and other trails are seemingly all obstacle. The path of least resistance, or *line*, is where you find it. In general, most obstacles are more challenging if you encounter them while climbing than while descending. On the other hand, in heavy surf (e.g., boulder fields, tangles of downfall, cliffs), fear plays a larger role when facing downhill.

Realize, too, that different riders have different strengths and weaknesses. Some folks can scramble over logs and boulders without a grunt, but they crash head over heels on every switchback turn. Some fly off the steepest drops and others freeze. Some riders climb like the wind and others just blow...and walk.

The key to overcoming "technical difficulties" is practice. Keep trying. Follow a rider who makes it look easy, and don't hesitate to ask for constructive criticism. Try shifting your weight (good riders move a lot, front to back, side to side, and up and down) and experimenting with balance and momentum. Find a smooth patch of lawn and practice riding as slowly as possible, even balancing at a standstill in a "track stand" (described in the Glossary). This will give you more confidence—and more time to recover or bail out—the next time the trail rears up and bites.

Charlton Lake Loop

Location: 40 miles southwest of Bend at Little Cultus Lake.

Distance: 18.1-mile loop.

Time: 2.5 to 4 hours.

Elevation gain: 2,200 feet.

Tread: 13.8 miles on singletrack; 4.3 miles on doubletrack.

Season: Early summer through fall.

Aerobic level: Strenuous. If the frequent short, steep climbs don't burn your legs, the long, steady climbs will.

Technical difficulty: 4. Numerous rocky sections and steep downhills.

Hazards: Fairly remote and lightly traveled trail system. Check with the USDA Forest Service to make sure trails 19.2 and 18.1

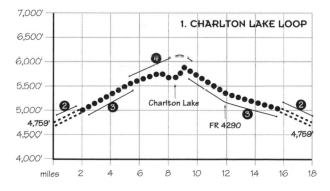

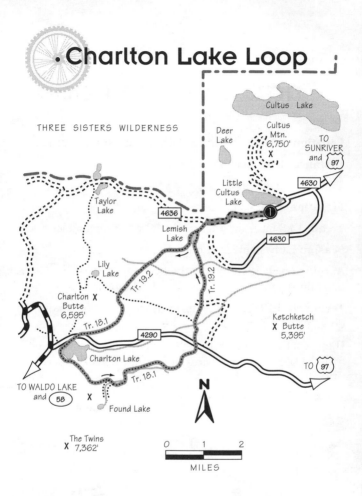

Charlton Lake Loop

THREE SISTERS WILDERNESS

Cultus Lake

Deer Lake

Cultus Mtn. 6,750' X

TO SUNRIVER and 97

Little Cultus Lake

4630

Taylor Lake

4636

4630

Lemish Lake

Tr. 19.2

Tr. 19.2

Lily Lake

Charlton Butte X 6,595'

Ketchketch X Butte 5,395'

Tr. 18.1

4290

Charlton Lake

TO 97

TO WALDO LAKE and 58

X

Tr. 18.1

Found Lake

N

The Twins X 7,362'

0   1   2

MILES

have been cleared. Mosquitoes can be thick in early summer. Bikes are not allowed on the Pacific Crest Trail.

Highlights: Expect little traffic on this fun singletrack, which stays firm even during the dusty days of summer. If you do collect a little dust, knock it off with a swim in the clear, blue waters of Charlton Lake.

Land status: Deschutes National Forest, Bend District.

Maps: Mountain Biking Central Oregon.

Access: From Bend drive 15 miles south on U.S. Highway 97 to the Sunriver exit. Turn right onto County Road 40 and drive about 20 miles west to the Cascade Lakes Highway, Oregon Highway 46. Turn left onto OR 46 and go about 1 mile. Turn right onto the Cultus and Little Cultus lakes access road, then turn left on gravel Forest Road 4630 and drive to Little Cultus Lake. Follow the road around the lake to the left and park at the second boat ramp.

The ride:

0.0   Start by pedaling west along the access road, which is now Forest Road 4636, toward Irish and Taylor lakes. This doubletrack rolls along through dense alpine forest with few technical challenges.

0.4   The road splits. Stay left on FR 4636.

2.0   Watch for the Lemish Lake Trailhead on the left. The trailhead is marked by a sign and small pullout. Gear down and pedal up the trail, which begins climbing more steeply.

2.6   Lemish Lake junction. It's best to complete this loop by going counterclockwise, so take the right-hand trail. The trail skirts west of Lemish Lake, climbing moderately over numerous small obstacles.

5.5 Four-way trail intersection. Go straight here to continue the Charlton Lake Loop. The trail immediately angles steeply uphill. (A left at this intersection leads to Clover Meadow and the Lemish Lake Loop, Ride 2. A right turn leads into a recent burn, and the route is not maintained.)

7.6 Junction with gravel FR 4290. The trail continues on the other side.

8.0 Welcome to Charlton Lake. The trail wraps counter-clockwise around the lake with good access for swimming or just relaxing.

8.5 To continue the loop, look for the trail as it climbs steeply away from the south end of the lake. Drop into your granny gear for this climb. The trail rolls over a series of climbs and descents to the next junction.

9.5 Immediately after a small creek crossing watch for a trail junction. Take the left-hand trail, which parallels and eventually crosses the creek again.

9.8 Splash across the creek once more.

10.2 Pass Round Meadow on the right. The next couple of miles offer fun, fast downhill.

11.9 Cross a faint doubletrack.

12.2 Cross gravel FR 4290.

12.7 Cross a small stream and roll up to Clover Meadow junction. Continue straight to finish the Charlton Lake Loop.

13.4 Cross another faint doubletrack.

13.6 Small creek crossing.

15.5 Return to Lemish Lake junction. Go right, retracing your tracks to FR 672.

16.1 Turn right on FR 672.

18.1 Back at the start.

Lemish Lake Loop

Location: 40 miles southwest of Bend at Little Cultus Lake.

Distance: 13.4 miles.

Time: 1.5 to 3 hours.

Elevation gain: 1,200 feet.

Tread: 9.4 miles on singletrack; 4 miles on doubletrack.

Season: Summer through fall.

Aerobic level: Moderate, with many short and sometimes steep climbs.

Technical difficulty: 3+, with many rocky sections and some steep downhills.

Hazards: Fairly remote and lightly traveled trail system. Check with the USDA Forest Service before riding to make sure this

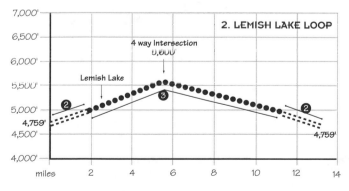

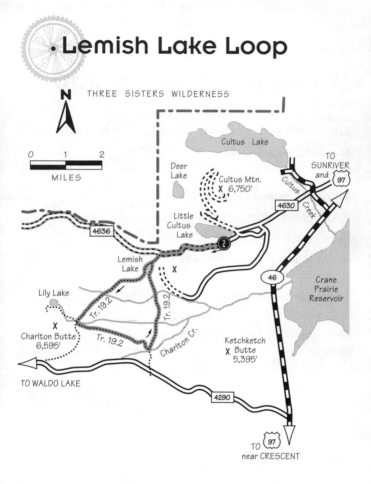

Lemish Lake Loop

THREE SISTERS WILDERNESS

N

0 1 2
MILES

Cultus Lake

Deer Lake

Cultus Mtn.
X 6,750'

Little Cultus Lake

TO SUNRIVER and 97

4630

Cultus Creek

4636

Lemish Lake

X

Tr. 19.2

Tr. 19.2

Tr. 19.2

Charlton Cr.

Lily Lake

Charlton Butte 6,595'

46

Crane Prairie Reservoir

Ketchketch X Butte 5,395'

TO WALDO LAKE

4290

TO 97 near CRESCENT

trail has been cleared. In early summer the mosquitoes will bite anything that moves, including your bike.

Highlights: Fun singletrack that doesn't get dusty in the summer. Enjoy an après-ride swim in Little Cultus Lake.

Land status: Deschutes National Forest, Bend District.

Maps: Mountain Biking Central Oregon.

Access: From Bend drive 15 miles south on U.S. Highway 97 to the Sunriver exit. Turn right and drive 20 miles west on County Road 40 to Cascade Lakes Highway 46. Turn left and go about 1 mile to the Cultus and Little Cultus lakes access road. Turn left on gravel Forest Road 4630 to Little Cultus Lake. Follow the road around the lake to the left and park at the second boat ramp.

The ride:

0.0   Start by pedaling west on the access road, which is now Forest Road 4636, toward Irish and Taylor lakes. This doubletrack rolls along through dense alpine forest with few technical challenges.

0.4   The road splits. Stay left on FR 4636.

2.0   Watch for the Lemish Lake Trailhead on the left, marked by a sign and small pullout. Ride up the trail, which begins climbing more steeply.

2.6   Lemish Lake junction. It's best to complete this loop by going counterclockwise, so take the right-hand trail. The trail skirts west of Lemish Lake, climbing moderately over numerous small obstacles.

5.5   Four-way trail intersection. Go left here to continue the Lemish Lake Loop. (Going straight leads to Charlton Lake and continues the Charlton Lake Loop, Ride 1. Don't go right here—it climbs steeply toward the Pacific Crest Trail and a recently burned area.)

5.7 After climbing a steep, short slope, the trail rolls down a long ridgeline for the next few miles.

7.3 Cross a faint doubletrack.

7.5 Cross the doubletrack again.

8.0 Clover Meadow junction. Ride left to continue the Lemish Lake Loop through dense young lodgepole pines.

8.7 Cross another faint doubletrack.

8.9 Small creek crossing.

10.8 Return to Lemish Lake junction. Go right to retrace your tracks back to FR 4630.

11.4 Go right on FR 4630.

13.4 Back at the trailhead. Little Cultus Lake sure looks inviting.

Cultus Loop

Location: The high lakes country, 40 miles southwest of Bend.

Distance: 12-mile loop.

Time: 1.5 to 3 hours.

Elevation gain: 1,000 feet.

Tread: 7.4 miles on singletrack; 3.4 miles on gravel road; 1.2 miles on paved road.

Season: Late spring through fall.

Aerobic level: Moderate.

Technical difficulty: 3. Watch for waterbars and roots.

Hazards: Expect some horse and foot traffic along Cultus Lake. Save the chiliburgers at the resort restaurant for *after* your ride.

Highlights: Great singletrack that doesn't get too dusty. After riding, go for a swim at the west end of Cultus Lake, then replenish your engery with lunch at Cultus Lake Resort. This entire route is well signed.

Land status: Deschutes National Forest, Bend District.

Maps: Mountain Biking Central Oregon.

Access: From Bend drive 13 miles south on U.S. Highway 97 to the Sunriver exit. Turn right and drive 20 miles west on County Road 40 to the Cascade Lakes Highway, Oregon Highway 46. Turn left, go about 1 mile, and turn right onto the Cultus and Little Cultus lakes access road (Forest Road 4635). Drive about 1 mile and park at the day use area just past the turnoff for Cultus Lake Resort.

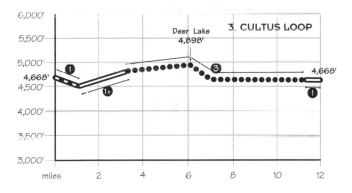

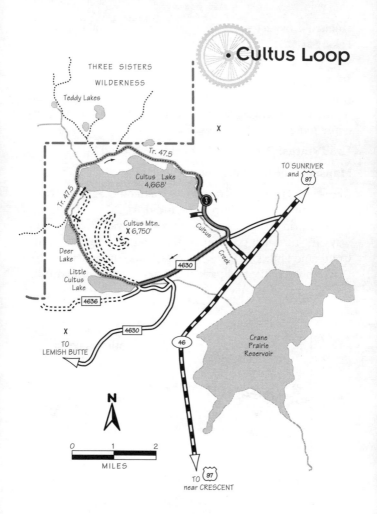

Cultus Loop

THREE SISTERS
WILDERNESS

Teddy Lakes

X

Tr. 47.5

Cultus Lake
4,668'

3

TO SUNRIVER
and 97

Tr. 475

Cultus Creek

Cultus Mtn.
X 6,750'

Deer
Lake

Little
Cultus
Lake

4630

4636

4630

X
TO
LEMISH BUTTE

46

Crane
Prairie
Reservoir

N

0   1   2
MILES

TO 97
near CRESCENT

24

The ride:

0.0   Pedal back down paved Forest Road 4635 to gravel Forest Road 4630.

1.0   Turn right on FR 4630. Follow this road 2.4 miles to Little Cultus Lake. The going can be bumpy due to severe washboards—grin and bear it. The grade starts off at a gradual climb but becomes steeper as you near Little Cultus Lake.

3.4   Junction at Little Cultus Lake. Go right on the road paralleling the north shoreline toward Deer Lake.

3.8   Trailhead parking lot on the left. Look for a sign for the Deer Lake Trail. The trail disappears among some dispersed campsites. Look for singletrack that begins next to a large log intended to keep vehicles off the trail.

3.9   Singletrack continues on the left and begins a rolling climb along Little Cultus Lake to Deer Lake.

5.5   That's Deer Lake on the left; follow the trail straight.

5.8   The route approaches a parking area for Deer Lake. Look for singletrack going left.

6.1   Trail junction. Go right; left heads into the Three Sisters Wilderness, which is closed to bikes. Begin a fun downhill section complete with waterbar jumps and banked corners.

6.7   Just as you think you're getting the hang of this downhill thing a super sharp left turn comes up without warning. Feather those brakes! With too much speed you will become a human pinball bouncing off lodgepole pine bumpers. Tilt.

7.2   Junction with an old section of doubletrack. Go left here and notice the west end of Cultus Lake. Take some time to explore this beach and campground; the clear waters make for a refreshing dip on hot days. There is no road access to this campground, so all campers come in by boat, foot, or bike. The remainder of the loop loosely follows the contours of the lake, going clockwise.

7.6 Trail junction; go right. The remaining 3.6 miles roughly follow the north shoreline of Cultus Lake. Stay right at all intersections.

8.0 Cross a bridge over a small stream.

8.5 Trail junction; stay straight. A left here leads to Winopee Lake in the Three Sisters Wilderness (no bikes allowed).

9.2 Trail junction; stay right.

11.1 Trail junction; bear right here toward the campground.

11.2 Cultus Lake Campground. Follow the gravel campground roads toward the exit and the day-use area.

11.8 Roll onto the paved access road, going right toward the day-use area.

12.0 End. Head over to the resort for a cold drink or food on the patio overlooking the lake.

Edison-Lava Trail

Location: 22 miles west of Bend, due south of Mount Bachelor.

Distance: 20.8 miles out and back.

Time: 2.5 to 5 hours.

Elevation gain: 2,600 feet.

Tread: 20.2 miles on singletrack; 0.6 mile on rough doubletrack.

Season: Summer through fall.

Aerobic level: Strenuous.

Technical difficulty: 4+.

Hazards: Exposed lava beds, log crossings, loose tread.

Highlights: Fast, technical singletrack; views from Lava lake; swimming in Little Lava Lake. The route is well signed.

Land status: Deschutes National Forest, Bend District.

Maps: Mountain Biking Central Oregon

Access: From Bend drive 16 miles west on Oregon Highway 46. Turn left onto Oregon Highway 45 (the Sunriver access road to Mount Bachelor) and continue 6 miles. Park at the Edison Snowpark, a total of 22 miles west of Bend.

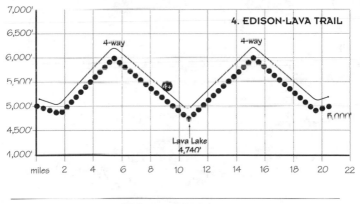

The ride:

0.0 Look for the trail sign at the south end of the parking area. The mileages on the sign are *not* correct. As the route traverses exposed lava beds you'll see many signs for cross-country ski trails. Ignore these and stay on the marked bike route.

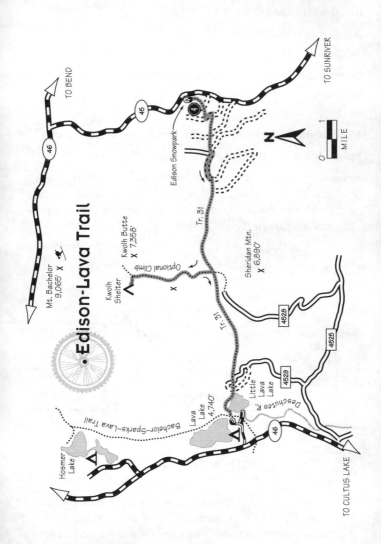

Edison-Lava Trail

TO BEND

46

45

Mt. Bachelor
9,065' X

46

Kwolh Butte
X 7,358'

Kwolh
Shelter

Optional Climb

X

Tr. 31

Edison Snowpark

4

TO SUNRIVER

N

0   1
MILE

Sheridan Mtn.
X 6,890'

Tr. 31

4528

4525

Hosmer
Lake

Bachelor-Sparks-Lava Trail

Lava Lake
4,740'

Little
Lava
Lake

4529

Deschutes R.

46

TO CULTUS LAKE

1.0   Cross doubletrack.

1.4   Trail becomes doubletrack. Go left down the hill.

1.5   Rejoin singletrack on the right. The trail begins climbing steeply and features a couple of rideable log crossings.

2.1   Cross doubletrack.

2.3   Join rough doubletrack going right.

2.5   Look for singletrack beginning again on the right. The next 7.9 miles to Lava Lake are singletrack. The first 3.1 miles are one continuous climb.

2.6   Cross doubletrack

5.6   Four-way intersection at saddle; go straight. The trail begins its descent here to the Lava Lakes. Be aware of unstable rocks, loose tread, and tight corners. (The trails to the right and left are predominantly ATV trails, though the trail on the right to Kwohl Butte Shelter is fun and offers an incredible view from the top. This option adds another 3 miles or so and 1,000 feet of steep climbing.)

9.1   Cross gravel road.

9.2   Cross faint doubletrack.

9.3   That's Little Lava Lake on the left. This small lake's clear blue waters are great for swimming on hot days.

10.3 Junction with Bachelor-Sparks-Lava Trail. Stay left around the south shoreline of Lava Lake directly ahead.

10.4 Lava Lake. There is a small store around the shoreline to the left and fresh water in the campground. To complete the ride follow your tire tracks back the way you came. A long loop is possible using this trail, Oregon Highway 45 and Oregon Highway 46, and the Bachelor-Sparks-Lava Trail. (See Ride 5.) Crank it counterclockwise.

20.8 Back at the trailhead.

Bachelor-Sparks-Lava Loop

Location: West of Bend in the high lakes area.

Distance: 28-mile loop on singletrack and pavement or 25 miles out and back on singletrack. Distance and climbing can be shortened by starting at the Sparks Lake Trailhead, or by taking the Quinn Meadow cutoff.

Time: 3 to 5 hours.

Elevation gain: 2,000 feet.

Tread: 12.4 miles on singletrack; 15.6 miles on pavement.

Season: Summer and fall.

Aerobic level: Moderate. Lots of climbing, but most of it is gradual.

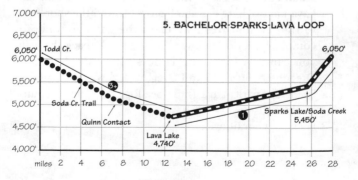

Technical difficulty: 3+, with log hops, loose tread, and many lava outcroppings.

Hazards: Plentiful rocky outcroppings demand strong technical skills to maneuver through and over. Most of this route is a long distance from any road, so carry a complete repair kit.

Highlights: Fun blend of technical and fast singletrack, mountain views, and Lava Lake.

Land status: Deschutes National Forest, Bend District.

Maps: Mountain Biking Central Oregon.

Access: From Bend drive 22 miles west toward Mount Bachelor on Oregon Highway 46. Look for the gravel road across from Forest Road 370 and the Todd Lake turnoff. Park at the first wide spot on this lightly traveled road.

The ride:

0.0   Ride west down the gravel road past a rock quarry on the right.

0.8   At a second quarry, watch for the trailhead on the left next to Todd Creek. A small sign and yellow diamonds in the trees mark the trail, which is a section of the Metolius-Windigo Trail. The trail begins fast and furious as it rolls generally downhill toward the Northwest Express Quad chairlift on Mount Bachelor. The route crosses several cross country ski trails over the first few miles—be careful to stay on the biking trail. It's the more obvious route; yellow diamond blazes mark the way.

1.7   Trail junction; stay right. (The left-hand trail leads up toward the Mount Bachelor Nordic Center.) Begin a series of moderately steep descents with tight corners.

4.1   Trail junction; go left toward the Quinn Meadow and

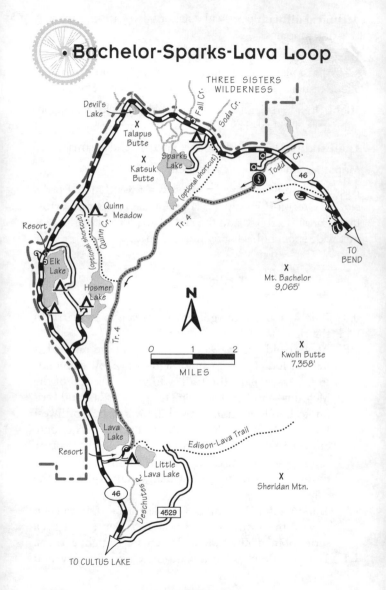

Bachelor-Sparks-Lava Loop

THREE SISTERS
WILDERNESS

Devil's
Lake

Fall Cr.

Soda Cr.

X
Talapus
Butte

Sparks
Lake

X
Katsuk
Butte

(optional shortcut)

Todd Cr.

46

S

TO
BEND

Quinn
Meadow

(optional shortcut)

Quinn Cr.

Tr. 4

Resort

Elk
Lake

Hosmer
Lake

X
Mt. Bachelor
9,065'

Tr. 4

N

0   1   2

MILES

X
Kwolh Butte
7,358'

Lava
Lake

Edison-Lava Trail

Resort

46

Little
Lava Lake

X
Sheridan Mtn.

Deschutes R.

4529

TO CULTUS LAKE

Lava Lake junction. The next 8.3 miles follow Trail 4 as marked by Forest Service route guides. (A right here makes a much shorter loop to the Sparks Lake/Soda Creek Trailhead, which is 3 miles away over fun, rolling terrain and a 2.2-mile paved climb back to your car.)

4.5 Trail junction; stay left. (The faint trail going right dead-ends in 0.25 mile at a nice view from the south end of Sparks Lake.

5.2 Hold on for a short series of waterbar drops down a steep slope.

7.1 Trail junction; stay left to continue to Lava Lake. (The trail right leads to Quinn Meadow and is a shorter loop option, 16.5 miles total.)

8.3 The trail winds through a large lava flow.

9.0 Begin a series of climbs and descents as the trail begins to drop down to Lava Lake.

10.9 North end of Lava Lake. The trail hugs the east shoreline and rolls into a few short technical sections. If you're ready for a swim, wait for the much clearer water of Little Lava Lake at the southeast end of Lava Lake.

12.4 Junction with the Edison-Lava Trail (see Ride 4). Turn right along the south shore of Lava Lake toward the campground and resort area.

12.6 Lava Lake Store and Resort. This is a great place to grab a snack and relax. For the out-and-back option, turn around here and retrace your tracks along Trail 4 back to your car. To complete the loop on pavement, follow the Lava Lake access road out to the Cascade Lakes Highway (Oregon Highway 46).

13.6 Cascade Lake Highway. Go right on this wide-shouldered road. Watch for traffic, which is moderate during summer.

20.8 Access road to Quinn Meadow Trailhead on the right.

Stay straight.

25.8 Access road to Sparks Lake/Soda Creek Trailhead on the right. Stay straight.

28.0 Turn right onto the gravel road and pedal down to your car.

Todd Lake to Three Creeks Lake Traverse

Location: 22 miles west of Bend, 2 miles past Mount Bachelor on the Cascade Lakes Highway (Oregon Highway 46).

Distance: 28.4 miles out and back.

Time: 3.5 to 6 hours.

Elevation gain: 3,600 feet.

Tread: 26.6 miles on doubletrack jeep road; 1.8 miles on gravel road.

Season: Midsummer through early fall.

Aerobic level: Strenuous. Expect long steady climbs but nothing exceptionally steep.

Technical difficulty: 3. Lots of rocky and rutted sections, but the route is wide enough to avoid most of these.

Hazards: Though weather should be a concern each time you ride, extra caution is recommended on this ride due to high elevations and exposure. Also, the route is open to motor vehicles, so watch for four-wheel drives with tread big enough to

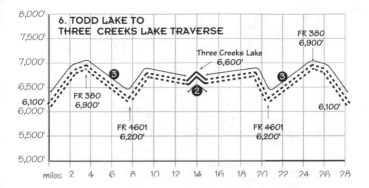

swallow mountain bikers whole. The rough terrain keeps traffic from going too fast, but be wary, especially when blazing downhill.

Highlights: A classic central Oregon ride with incredible high alpine scenery, wildflowers, and creek crossings. Forest Road 370 climbs higher than any other in the Cascades.

Land status: Deschutes National Forest, Bend and Sisters districts.

Maps: Mountain Biking Central Oregon.

Access: From Bend drive 22 miles west on Oregon Highway 46 to Forest Road 370 on the right, signed for Todd Lake. Park at the lot for the Todd Lake Trailhead, about 0.5 mile up the road.

The ride:

0.0   From the Todd Lake parking area begin riding up Forest Road 370, the route for all but 1.8 miles of this ride. The climbing starts out steep for the first 2.3 miles.

35

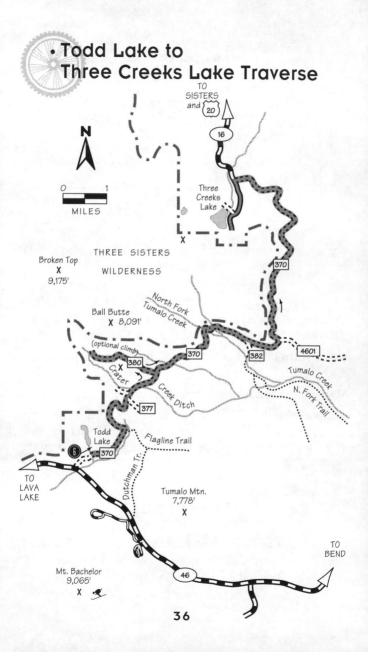

• Todd Lake to
Three Creeks Lake Traverse

N

0   1
MILES

TO
SISTERS
and 20

16

Three
Creeks
Lake

370

THREE SISTERS

Broken Top
X
9,175'

WILDERNESS

Ball Butte
X 8,091'

North Fork
Tumalo Creek

(optional climb)

380
X

4601

370

382

Crater

Tumalo Creek

Creek Ditch

N. Fork Trail

377

Todd
Lake

Flagline Trail

6   370

Dutchman Tr.

TO
LAVA
LAKE

Tumalo Mtn.
7,778'
X

TO
BEND

Mt. Bachelor
9,065'
X

46

36

1.5 Route crosses the Big Meadow. The frequent orange and blue signs about 10 to 12 feet above the ground mark snowmobile and cross-country ski routes, respectively.

2.3 Bachelor overlook on the right, with spectacular views of Mount Bachelor and Tumalo Mountain. The road levels off here, traversing alpine meadows covered with wildflowers during the summer. The scenery begins to open to the west with views of Broken Top and South Sister in the background and several lesser peaks in the foreground.

2.6 FR 377 on your right; continue straight on FR 370.

2.7 FR 378 goes left; continue straight on FR 370.

2.9 Crater Creek Ditch. Although it looks like any high mountain stream, this is actually a diversion canal into the Bridge Creek Watershed. Begin climbing again to the junction with FR 380.

3.5 FR 380 goes left; continue right on FR 370. (FR 380 climbs to the Soda Creek Trailhead and the Three Sisters Wilderness boundary. This is a nice spur route for even better views of the surrounding mountains and desert lands to the east. Riding this up-and-back option adds about 2 miles and 400 feet of climbing.)

3.7 Begin a long descent into Happy Valley. Expect several rocky sections, some tight corners, a creek crossing or two, and—sure enough—a happy feeling at the bottom.

6.8 FR 382 goes right; stay straight. This marks the end of the long descent, so gear down for the climb ahead. (FR 382 leads to the upper trailhead of the North Fork Trail; see Ride 11.)

7.7 Forest Road 4601 goes right; bear left to stay on FR 370 and continue climbing. (FR 4601 leads down to the Bridge Creek Burn and back to Bend.)

9.3 Finish the long climb and enjoy some rolling terrain.

13.3 Junction with FR 16; go left toward Three Creeks Lake. A short steady climb leads to the basin of Three Creeks

Lake beneath the ramparts of Tam McArthur Rim.

14.2 Three Creeks Lake. Take a well-deserved break here before heading back along the same route.

28.4 Back where you started at the Todd Lake Trailhead.

Swampy Lakes Loop

Location: 16 miles west of Bend on the Cascade Lakes Highway (Oregon Highway 46).

Distance: 4.3-mile loop.

Time: 30 minutes to 1 hour.

Elevation gain: 300 feet.

Tread: 3.6 miles on singletrack; 0.7 mile on doubletrack.

Season: Early summer through fall.

Aerobic level: Easy.

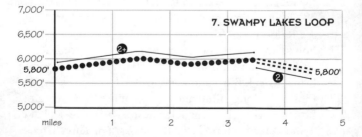

Technical difficulty: 2+.

Hazards: Various rocky or loose sandy sections; log crossings.

Highlights: Rolling singletrack, views of Swampy Lakes through trees. The route is well signed.

Land status: Deschutes National Forest, Bend District.

Maps: Mountain Biking Central Oregon.

Access: From Bend drive 16 miles west on the Cascade Lakes Highway (Oregon Highway 46). Park at the signed Swampy Lakes Snowpark on the right side of the road.

The ride:

0.0 Look for the singletrack beginning across from the restrooms.

0.05 Trail to Vista Butte and shelter goes left; continue straight.

0.1 Trail junction. Go left and begin a gentle climb.

0.7 Trail steepens briefly as it winds through a small rock garden.

1.0 Junction with the Swampy Lakes Tie Trail; stay straight.

1.5 A faint trail goes right; stay straight. Begin a steep descent to the Swampy Lakes, barely visible through the trees.

2.0 Cross a small log bridge and roll to an intersection with the Flagline Trail (see Ride 11) and then the South Fork Trail. Follow the Swampy Lakes Trail right (east).

2.1 Pedal straight, past the Swampy Lakes cross-country ski shelter. Roll onto a short section of new trail that is windy and narrow.

2.3 Slow for a creek crossing. This might be rideable, but the penalty for failure is a rock to the nose or worse.

• Swampy Lakes Loop

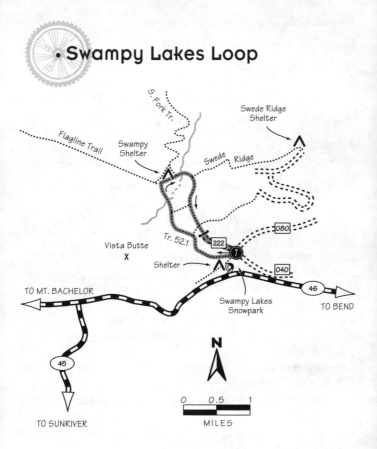

S. Fork Tr.

Swede Ridge Shelter

Flagline Trail

Swampy Shelter

Swede Ridge

Vista Butte
X

Tr. 52.1

222

080

Shelter

7

040

TO MT. BACHELOR

Swampy Lakes Snowpark

46

TO BEND

45

TO SUNRIVER

N

0   0.5   1

MILES

2.6 The Swede Ridge Trail goes left (see Ride 8). Stay straight on less defined trail.

2.8 The Swampy Lakes Tie Trail goes right; stay straight. Pump up a short hill, then coast.

3.3 Go straight through a four-way trail intersection at a clearing in the trees.

3.4 Go around a gate, then pedal straight on doubletrack. Enjoy a fun descent back to the trailhead, but be careful of loose tread.

4.1 Another four-way junction; go right on singletrack.

4.2 Singletrack goes right; stay straight.

4.3 Back at the trailhead.

Swede Ridge Loop

Location: 16 miles west of Bend on the Cascade Lakes Highway (Oregon Highway 46).

Distance: 8.2-mile loop.

Time: 1 to 2 hours.

Elevation gain: 800 feet.

Tread: 6.6 miles on singletrack; 1.6 miles on doubletrack.

Season: Early summer through fall.

Aerobic level: Moderate

Technical difficulty: 3.

·Swede Ridge Loop

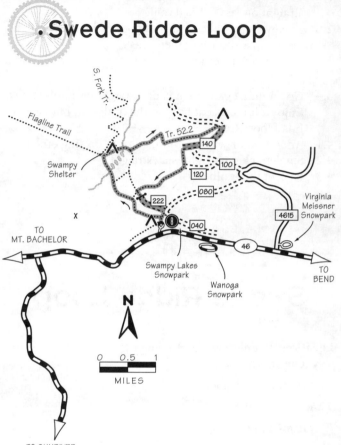

S. Fork Tr.

Flagline Trail

Tr. 52.2

140

100

120

080

222

Swampy
Shelter

X

4615

Virginia
Meissner
Snowpark

TO
MT. BACHELOR

040

46

TO
BEND

Swampy Lakes
Snowpark

Wanoga
Snowpark

N

0   0.5   1
MILES

TO SUNRIVER

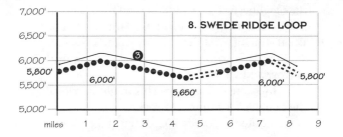

Hazards: Rocky sections and log crossings.

Highlights: Rolling singletrack, views from Swede Ridge Shelter. The route is well signed.

Land Status: Deschutes National Forest, Bend District.

Maps: Mountain Biking Central Oregon.

Access: From Bend drive 16 miles west on the Cascade Lakes Highway (Oregon Highway 46) and park at the Swampy Lakes Snowpark on the right side of the road.

The ride:

0.0 Look for the singletrack beginning across from the snowpark restrooms.

0.05 Trail to Vista Butte and shelter goes left; continue straight.

0.1 Trail junction. Go left and begin a gentle climb.

0.7 Trail steepens briefly as it winds through a small rock garden.

1.0 Junction with the Swampy Lakes Tie Trail; stay straight.

1.5 A faint trail goes right; stay straight. Begin a steep descent to the Swampy Lakes, barely visible through the trees.

2.0 Cross a small log bridge and roll to an intersection with

43

the Flagline Trail (see Ride 11) and then the South Fork Trail. Follow the Swampy Lakes Trail right (east).

2.1 Pedal straight, past the Swampy Lakes cross-country ski shelter. Roll onto a short section of new trail that is narrow and windy.

2.3 Slow for a creek crossing. This might be rideable, but the penalty for failure is a rock to the melon or worse.

2.6 Go left onto the Swede Ridge Trail and begin a series of short climbs and descents as the trail traverses the ridge.

4.5 Turn right and descend on Forest Road 100. The Swede Ridge Shelter is downhill to the left. It's a nice place to take a break, with a spectacular view across the valley to the Bridge Creek Burn and Broken Top in the background.

5.2 Locked gate. Forest Road 100 goes left. Instead, go around the gate and head west on FR 140, which has reverted to doubletrack.

5.4 The doubletrack ends. Go left on singletrack.

5.7 FR 120 goes left; veer right and begin climbing. It can get steep.

7.2 Roll up to a four-way trail intersection at the edge of a large clearing. Go left.

7.3 Go around a gate and enjoy a fun doubletrack descent.

8.0 Another four-way intersection. Go right on singletrack.

8.1 Swampy Lakes Trail goes left; stay straight.

8.2 Back at the snowpark.

Tangent Loop

Location: 13 miles west of Bend on the Cascade Lakes Highway (Oregon Highway 46).

Distance: 5.8-mile loop.

Time: 1 to 1.5 hours.

Elevation gain: 700 feet.

Tread: 3.1 miles on gravel road; 2.7 miles on doubletrack.

Season: Summer through fall.

Aerobic level: Easy to moderate.

Technical difficulty: 1+ to -2.

Hazards: Loose sections, short section of washboard on gravel descent.

Highlights: Rolling doubletrack through subalpine forests. It's easy to hook up with other trails to make longer rides. The route is well signed.

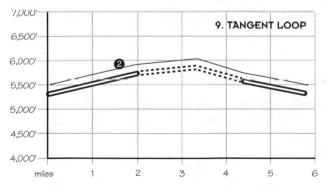

•Tangent Loop

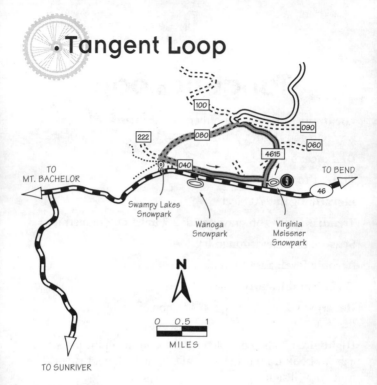

Land status: Deschutes National Forest, Bend District.

Maps: Mountain Biking Central Oregon.

Access: From Bend drive 13 miles west on OR 46 and park at the Virginia Meissner Snopark on the right side of the road.

The ride:

0.0   Pedal north and west on gravel Forest Road 4615 over some washboard and moderately steep climbs.

1.7   Turn left on Forest Road 080, which climbs gently toward Swampy Lakes Snowpark.

3.1   Nordeen cross-country ski loop goes left; stay straight.

3.4   At a four-way intersection go left on Forest Road 222. (Straight on singletrack leads to Swampy Lakes Snowpark.) This is a good point to hook up with either the Swampy Lakes Loop (see Ride 7) or the Swede Ridge Loop (see Ride 8).

3.6   The road splits. Veer left on FR 040 and begin a long descent on packed dirt.

4.4   FR 040 turns to gravel. Hang on for a short but steep downhill that's usually washboarded.

5.7   Roll up to FR 4615 and turn right to drop back to the trailhead.

5.8   Back at the Snowpark.

Tangent–Quarry Site 1041 Loop

Location: 13 miles west of Bend on the Cascade Lakes Highway (Oregon Highway 46).

Distance: 12.4-mile loop.

Time: 1.5 to 3 hours.

Elevation gain: 1,300 feet.

Tread: 9 miles on gravel road; 3.4 miles on doubletrack.

Season: Late spring through fall.

Aerobic level: Moderate.

Technical difficulty: 2.

Hazards: Sections with loose tread; short sections of washboard on gravel descents. Also watch for spoke-eating sticks.

Highlights: Rolling doubletrack, subalpine forests, a nice view from Quarry Site 1041, chance of seeing wildlife. It's easy to hook up with other trails to make longer rides.

Land status: Deschutes National Forest, Bend District.

Maps: Mountain Biking Central Oregon.

Access: From Bend drive 13 miles west on the Cascade Lakes Highway (Oregon Highway 46) and park at the Virginia Meissner Snowpark on the right side of the road.

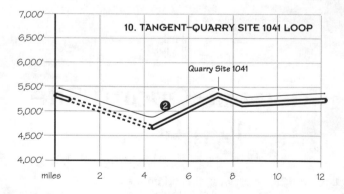

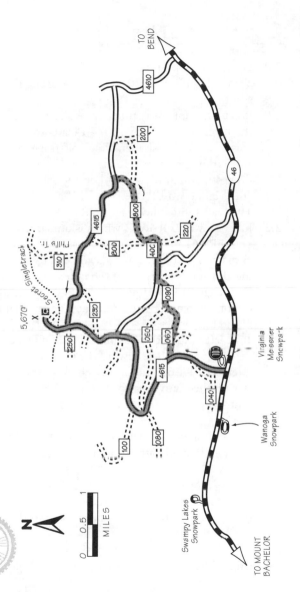

Tangent–Quarry Site 1041 Loop

N

MILES
0   0.5   1

TO BEND

4610

200

4615

600

Phil's Tr.

Secret Singletrack

310

300

250

230

X 5,670'

40C

220

090

46

067

050

4615

040

100

080

Virginia Meissner Snowpark

Wanoga Snowpark

Swampy Lakes Snowpark

TO MOUNT BACHELOR

49

The ride:

0.0   Pedal north on gravel Forest Road 4615.

0.8   Turn right onto FR 060 and begin a fast doubletrack descent.

1.0   Roll up to a four-way junction. A short ride and hike up the unmarked left-hand road leads to the Meissner cross-country ski shelter, which offers a nice view of the surrounding country. To stay on the main route, continue straight and downhill on FR 060.

1.7   Turn right onto FR 090.

2.1   The road splits. Stay left on FR 090.

2.2   Junction with FR 4612, which is unmarked. Turn right onto FR 4612.

2.4   Turn left onto FR 400 and stay on the main route, ignoring all spurs, for the next 0.6 mile.

3.0   Turn right at junction with FR 800. Get ready for an exciting downhill with some sketchy ruts that can suck in careless riders.

4.2   Turn left onto FR 4615 and begin a long steady climb that steepens a little toward the end. Several dirt roads intersect FR 4615 along the climb—ignore these and stay on the main drag for the next 2.8 miles.

7.0   Four-way intersection. Go right toward Quarry Site 1041.

7.1   Cross singletrack (which hooks into the top part of Phil's trail) and begin climbing more steeply toward the quarry site.

7.5   Quarry Site 1041. The nice view gets even better with a short hike to the top of the butte. After soaking in the scenery, turn around and head back to the four-way intersection at mile 7.0.

8.0   Four-way intersection again. Go straight.

9.0   Unmarked FR 4612 goes left; stay straight as the route begins to climb steadily for the next 1.5 miles.

10.5 FR 100 goes right; keep straight. (FR 100 leads to the Swede Ridge cross-country ski shelter—see Ride 8).

10.6 FR 090 goes left and FR 080 goes right. Keep straight on FR 4615.

12.4 Cruise back down to the Snowpark.

North Fork–Flagline Loop

Location: 13 miles west of Bend, beginning in the Bridge Creek Burn and heading up to the flanks of Broken Top Mountain

Distance: 20.6-mile loop.

Time: 2 to 4 hours.

Elevation gain: 2,800 feet.

Tread: 13.7 miles on singletrack; 6.9 miles on doubletrack.

Season: August 15 through early fall. The Oregon Department of Fish and Wildlife has issued a closure of the Flagline Trail until August 15 because it passes through sensitive elk rearing grounds. Check with the USDA Forest Service or local shops to get an update on this opening date. An early summer alternative to the Flagline portion would be to traverse south to Oregon Highway 46 on the new Dutchman Trail, and then return on the Swampy Lakes Trail to the South Fork Trail and back down to the trailhead (see Ride 38).

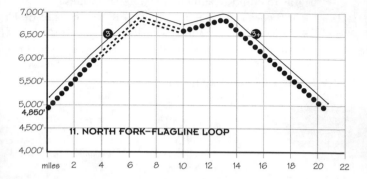

Aerobic level: Strenuous.

Technical difficulty: 3+.

Hazards: The South Fork Trail downhill demands respect. The higher sections of this route are exposed to weather, which can change quickly. Catching air over waterfalls is not recommended.

Highlights: Seven waterfalls along Tumalo Creek, high alpine scenery, fun singletrack descents, prime elk habitat.

Land status: Deschutes National Forest, Bend District.

Maps: Mountain Biking Central Oregon.

Access: From Bend drive or ride 13 miles west on Skyliner Drive, which becomes Forest Road 4603 and changes to gravel. Park at the Tumalo Falls picnic area and trailhead at the end of the road. Biking to the trailhead adds 26 road miles, making this a good half day's effort.

North Fork–Flagline Loop

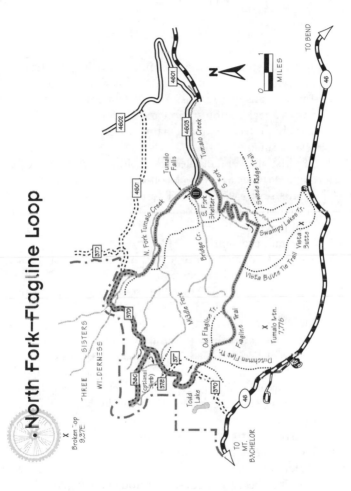

The ride:

0.0 Begin climbing steeply on singletrack toward Tumalo Falls.

0.1 The trail splits. Stay right on the North Fork Trail. Bridge Creek Trail, to the left, is closed to bikes.

0.2 Tumalo Falls overlook. Continue climbing as the trail passes a registration station and enters dense forest.

0.8 The climb steepens and remains strenuous for the next several miles.

2.0 The first of several marked viewpoints offers a good rest stop. More viewpoints to come overlook some of the route's seven waterfalls. There are also two bridged creek crossings.

3.5 Trail junction. Turn right.

3.7 Top Trailhead sign.

3.8 Turn right over the bridge and roll onto Forest Road 382, which climbs away from the creek.

4.3 Junction with FR 370 (see Ride 6). Turn left and begin climbing steeply for the next 3 miles or so.

7.6 FR 380 goes right and marks the end of climbing for a while. FR 380 offers an optional 1-mile climb to the Soda Creek Trailhead, which accesses Broken Top Mountain within the Three Sisters Wilderness. This side trip adds about 400 vertical feet and some spectacular views. To continue the main loop keep left on FR 370.

8.5 FR 378 goes right; keep straight.

8.6 FR 377 goes left; keep straight.

8.9 Watch for a great overlook of Mount Bachelor on the left. Then begin a fun descent through the Big Meadow to the Flagline Trail.

10.0 FR 370 continues dropping south, but watch for the trailhead for the Flagline Trail on the left. The trailhead is not currently marked and can be difficult to find. The trail begins at a small turnout on a corner in the road going left. You'll know it's the right trail if it immediately crosses a small creek.

10.3 The new Metolius–Windigo Trail goes left. Keep right.

10.4 The Metolius–Windigo Trail goes straight; bear left.

10.7 Junction with new trail coming in from Dutchman Flat on the right. Keep straight.

10.9 The trail splits. The new and recommended trail goes right and begins climbing more steeply. (The trail to the left is slated for closure and may be obliterated by press time.)

14.2 A side trail goes left to a small lake. Continue straight as the trail descends toward the old Flagline Trail.

15.4 The new trail grows faint for the final 20 yards before rejoining the old trail. Go right on these reunited trails as the route keeps descending.

15.7 Vista Butte Trail ties in from the right. Keep straight.

16.9 Junction with Swampy Lakes Trails. Take the left-most trail, which is the South Fork Trail and is the least defined.

17.1 Second junction with Swampy Lakes Trail at sign. Go straight on the South Fork Trail.

18.8 Junction with the Bridge Creek Trail. Go right and downhill along the creek.

19.9 South Fork cross-country ski shelter.

20.2 Junction with the Skyliner Trail. Go left.

20.5 Cross Bridge Creek.

20.6 Roll back into the Tumalo Falls parking area.

Skyliner Loop

Location: 10 miles west of Bend on Skyliner Road.

Distance: 13.6-mile loop.

Time: 1.5 to 3 hours.

Elevation gain: 1,500 feet.

Tread: 11 miles on singletrack; 2.6 miles on doubletrack.

Season: Summer through fall.

Aerobic level: Strenuous.

Technical difficulty: 3+.

Hazards: Switchbacks, some loose sections, roots and rocks. The beautiful scenery can derail distracted riders—it's better to stop and gawk.

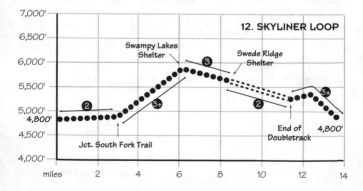

Highlights: Views of Tumalo Canyon, Broken Top, and Bridge Creek Burn.

Land status: Deschutes National Forest, Bend District.

Maps: Mountain Biking Central Oregon.

Access: From Bend drive or ride 10 miles west on paved Skyliner Drive and park at the Skyliner Snowplay Area on the left side of the road.

The ride:

0.0   Pedal on new singletrack that leaves from the trailhead sign on the west end of the parking area.

0.1   Cross a dirt road and begin climbing easily as the trail parallels the road.

0.4   Pass cabins on the right (part of the OMSI Summer Camp).

0.6   Go through a green gate and cross a small creek. Continue climbing on singletrack.

0.7   Junction with loop trail. Go right and begin a rolling section through the Bridge Creek Burn.

3.0   Junction with the South Fork Trail. Go left and re-enter the forest, climbing along the south fork of Bridge Creek.

3.3   South Fork cross-country ski shelter. From here the trail becomes more challenging with steeper inclines and many exposed roots and rocks.

4.5   Junction with the Bridge Creek Trail. Go left over the bridge and climb steeply out of the canyon.

6.0   Junction with the Swampy Lakes Trail (see Ride 7). Go left.

6.1   Swampy Lakes Shelter. Stay left on a new section of trail that twists and turns its way toward Swede Ridge.

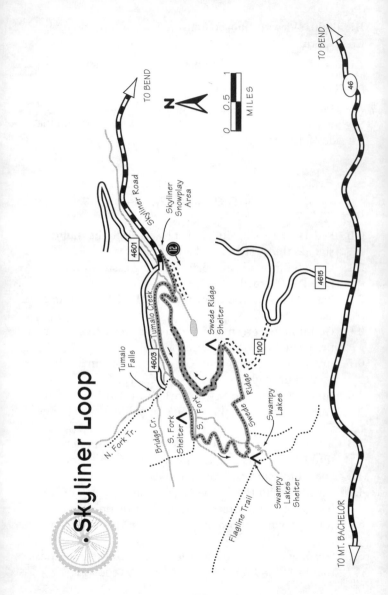

Skyliner Loop

TO BEND

TO BEND

N

0 0.5 1
MILES

Skyliner Road

Skyliner Snowplay Area

12

4601

Tumalo Creek

Tumalo Falls

4603

Swede Ridge Shelter

100

4615

N. Fork Tr.

Bridge Cr.

S. Fork Shelter

S. Fork

Swede Ridge

Swampy Lakes

Flagline Trail

Swampy Lakes Shelter

46

TO MT. BACHELOR

6.6　Junction with the Swede Ridge Trail. Hang a left and roll along the ridgetop.

8.6　Turn left onto Forest Road 100, which is doubletrack. (The Swede Ridge cross-country ski shelter is just down the hill on the right. It offers a good place for a break and the views are outstanding.)

11.2　Faint doubletrack goes left; keep straight. FR 100 soon ends and a small signpost marks the route, which follows a new section of singletrack.

11.3　Grunt up a short but steep climb.

11.8　The views begin to open up again as the trail descends the spine of the ridge to the first of two switchbacks.

12.8　Trail junction. Turn right and retrace the next 0.7 mile back to the trailhead at the Skyliner Snowplay Area.

12.9　Go through the gate and pick up the trail going left.

13.6　Back at the trailhead.

Skyliner-Tumalo Out and Back

Location: 10 miles west of Bend in Tumalo Creek Canyon.

Distance: 7.6-mile round trip.

Time: 1 to 1.5 hours.

Elevation gain: 600 feet.

Tread: 7.6 miles on singletrack.

Season: Late spring through fall.

Aerobic level: Easy to moderate. Not much climbing overall, but a couple of short steep ascents may jump-start your heart rate.

Technical difficulty: 2+.

Hazards: A few log hops and some loose tread. Be alert for kamikaze chipmunks.

Highlights: Great views, fun rolling singletrack, Tumalo Falls.

Land status: Deschutes National Forest, Bend District.

Maps: Mountain Biking Central Oregon.

Access: From Bend drive or ride 10 miles west on Skyliner Drive to the Skyliner Snowplay Area parking lot on the left side of the road. The trail is marked by a large sign.

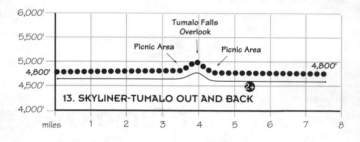

The ride:

0.0   Pedal on new singletrack that leaves from the trailhead sign on the west end of the parking area.
0.1   Cross a dirt road and begin climbing easily as the trail parallels the road. This portion of trail can be very dusty in the summer but is still easily rideable.
0.4   Pass cabins on the right (part of the Oregon Museum of Science and Industry [OMSI] Summer Camp).

Skyliner-Tumalo Out and Back

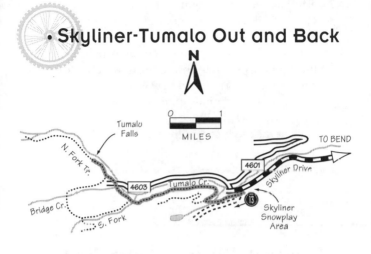

0.6 Go through a green gate and cross a small creek. Continue climbing on singletrack.

0.7 Junction with loop trail. Turn right toward Tumalo Falls. (Straight leads up a tough climb to the much longer and more difficult Skyliner Loop. See Ride 12.)

1.1 Trail junction. Go straight as the trail climbs over rolling terrain above Tumalo Creek. (The trail to the right goes to the OMSI Summer Camp and is closed to the general public.)

2.9 Bridge over the south fork of Bridge Creek.

3.0 Trail junction. Go right toward Tumalo Falls. (A left here puts you on the South Fork Trail, which climbs steeply to the Swampy Lakes trail system.)

3.5 Tumalo picnic area and parking for Tumalo Falls Trail. Look for the trail beginning again on the far end of the parking lot. Take it and gear down for the steep climb to the falls overlook.

3.7 Trail junction. Stay right to Tumalo Falls. (The Bridge Creek Trail, to the left, goes into the Bend watershed and is closed to bikes.)

3.8 Tumalo Falls overlook. Take a break here before returning on the same route or heading down the access road. The road is flatter but does get dusty and washboarded from cars. (Or continue uphill on singletrack to explore the North Fork Trail; see Ride 11.)

7.6 Back at the Skyliner Trailhead.

Bend Riverside Trail

Location: Near Deschutes River on the north side of Bend, leading to a canyon overlook with views of Mount Jefferson and ranchland to the north.

Distance: 5.9 miles out and back.

Time: 30 minutes to 1.5 hours.

Elevation gain: 150 feet.

Tread: 5.7 miles on 12-foot-wide, woodchip trail; 0.2 mile on pavement.

Season: Year-round.

Aerobic level: Easy.

Technical difficulty: 1+, with a couple of curb hops.

Hazards: Watch for other trail users, and trust your helmet to ward off any shanked golf balls from River's Edge Golf Course.

Highlights: This short ride close to town offers a nice overlook of the Deschutes River Canyon and views north of Mount Jefferson. Good access to Awbry Butte trails.

Land status: City of Bend.

Maps: Mountain Biking Central Oregon.

Access: In Bend, park at the end of NW First Street north of Portland Avenue.

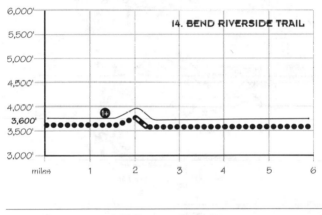

The ride:

0.0 Pedal through the gate at the end of First Street and head down river on the trail. The route is marked by blue signs over its entire length.

0.6 The trail splits; go left up the hill. Please stay off the grounds of the River's Edge Golf Course—the course and all cart paths are closed to bikes.

0.7 Junction with Mount Washington Drive. Turn right and head down the pavement to rejoin the trail on the left just after you cross the irrigation canal.

0.8 Turn left onto the trail again next to the irrigation canal.

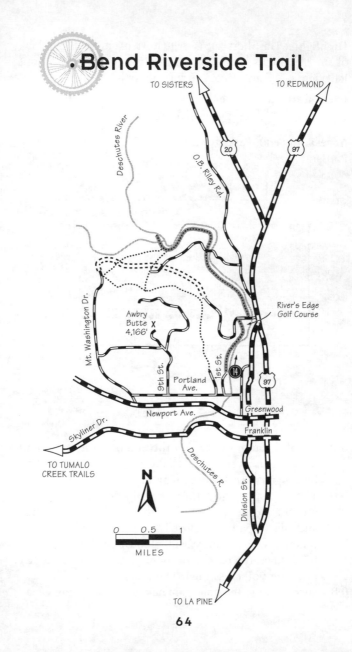

Bend Riverside Trail

TO SISTERS

TO REDMOND

Deschutes River

O.B. Riley Rd.

20

97

River's Edge
Golf Course

Awbry
Butte
4,166'

Mt. Washington Dr.

9th St.

Portland
Ave.

1st St.

14

97

Newport Ave.

Greenwood

Skyliner Dr.

Franklin

TO TUMALO
CREEK TRAILS

Deschutes R.

Division St.

N

0   0.5   1
MILES

TO LA PINE

1.9   Cross a paved road.

2.2   Cross another paved road. Views begin opening up to canyon and mountains.

2.8   Trail junction. Stay right and jam up a short climb to continue the Riverside Trail. (The singletrack heading uphill to the left leads into the ever-changing Awbry Butte trail system.)

2.95 A gate marks the end of the trail. The property behind the gate is private and the owners don't want bikers going through. Please respect their rights. Dismount and scramble down toward the canyon edge to view the river below. Return along the same route or access the Awbry Butte trail system to finish your ride.

5.9   Back at the trailhead.

Shevlin Park Loop

Location: 3 miles northwest of Bend along Tumalo Creek.

Distance: 12.4 miles. A shorter loop, beginning at Shevlin Park, is 4.8 miles.

Time: 2 hours. (30 minutes to 1.5 hours for just the Shevlin Park Loop.)

Elevation gain: 500 feet.

Tread: 4.5 miles on singletrack; 0.2 mile on doubletrack; 7.7 miles on pavement.

Season: All year, snowpack permitting.

Aerobic level: Easy to moderate.

Technical difficulty: 3. Mostly easy cruising with a couple of short technical sections.

Hazards: Watch for traffic on the road from Bend (ride on the wide shoulders). Also, beware the stairstep section just before reaching Tumalo Creek (when riding the loop clockwise). This trail sees heavy use from hikers, joggers, and cyclists, so ride in control and yield the right of way.

Highlights: Smooth, firm singletrack; beautiful old-growth forest; Tumalo Creek; picnic areas.

Land status: Bend Metro Parks.

Maps: Mountain Biking Central Oregon.

Access: Ride this one from town, starting in Bend at the Galveston Street bridge over the Deschutes River. (For a shorter, 4.8-mile loop, drive to the trailhead at Shevlin Park following the ride description below to mile 3.8.) Proceed west on Galveston to 14th, right on 14th to Newport, then left on Newport, which turns into Shevlin Park Road. The park is 3.8 miles on the left, where the road crosses Tumalo Creek. The trailhead is on the left next to entrance sign.

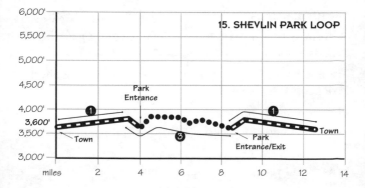

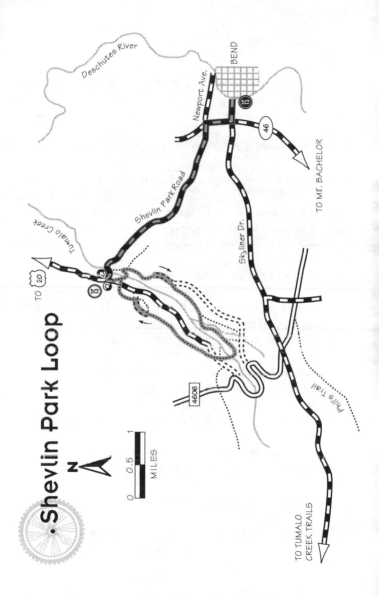

Shevlin Park Loop

TO TUMALO
CREEK TRAILS

Phil's Trail

4606

MILES
0   0.5   1

N

Deschutes River

BEND

Newport Ave.

15

46

TO MT. BACHELOR

Shevlin Park Road

Skyliner Dr.

Tumalo Creek

TO 20

15

The ride:

0.0 From the bridge over the Deschutes River, pedal west up Galveston Street to 14th Street. Turn right on 14th then left on Newport, which becomes Shevlin Park Road. Continue northwest until you reach Shevlin Park.

3.8 Park entrance on left. The trailhead is next to the entrance sign on the left.

3.9 Cross a footbridge over Tumalo Creek and head up singletrack that switchbacks steeply out of the canyon.

4.0 A trail goes left at the second switchback; stay right.

4.1 Another trail goes left; stay straight. As the trail breaks out of the canyon the grade eases and remains flat for a while.

4.7 Turn right onto doubletrack.

4.9 Turn right onto singletrack again and begin a fun section of swooping trail. Be alert for obstacles and hikers around *every* corner.

5.6 The trail forks. Follow the more defined route downhill to the right.

5.7 Cross a bridge over a small side creek and head up the steep, technical climb to the left.

6.1 Slow for a difficult stairstep descent.

6.2 Footbridge over Tumalo Creek. This is nice spot for a break.

6.3 Five-way intersection. Make a soft left (actually straight) to continue on the loop. The trail climbs easily and then rolls along the top of the canyon. (A hard right leads to a picnic area, while a hard left leads to Rd. 4606.

7.8 Just before the park maintenance lot hang on for a whoop-dee-do with a flat landing. Go straight, down the doubletrack. Ignore the trails going right—you'll join them shortly.

7.9   Veer left onto singletrack that climbs briefly and then drops to the bottom of the canyon.

8.5   Turn left onto the paved park access road.

8.6   Park exit. Go right on Shevlin Park Road toward Bend.

12.4 Back where you started on the bridge over the Deschutes on Galveston Street.

Phil's Trail: Long Loop

Location: Just west of Bend in the foothills leading up toward the Swampy Lakes area.

Distance: 22.8-mile loop beginning and ending at the Galveston Street bridge.

Time: 2 to 4 hours. (Shorter loops of about 1 hour are possible.)

Elevation gain: 1,600 feet.

Tread: 9.4 miles on singletrack; 9.4 miles on doubletrack; 1.8 miles on cinder, 2.2 miles on pavement.

Season: Spring, summer, fall.

Aerobic level: Moderate. Lots of climbing, but most of it is gradual.

Technical difficulty: 2+, except for singletrack above Forest Road 300, which rates up to a 4+.

Hazards: Boulder field below the "helicopter pad," loose dirt.

Numerous old doubletracks intersect the route (watch for brown bike signs). These side tracks are mentioned in the text only when the correct route is unclear.

Highlights: Incredible singletrack cruising through the forest, occasional views, lots of wildlife.

Land status: Deschutes National Forest, Bend District.

Maps: Mountain Biking Central Oregon.

Access: Pedal this one from Bend, beginning at the Galveston Street bridge over the Deschutes River. To drive to the trailhead, follow the ride description below to mile 3.8.

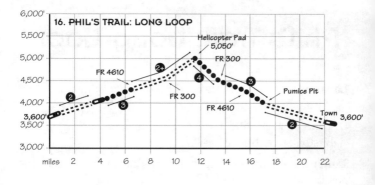

The ride:

- 0.0 From the Galveston Street bridge go west up Galveston, which becomes Skyliner Road after a four-way stop as it leaves town.
- 0.7 Just after a pumice pit on the left, drop onto doubletrack that parallels Skyliner Road.
- 2.4 Powerline doubletrack goes left; continue straight.
- 2.8 Follow gravel road to left (not doubletrack).

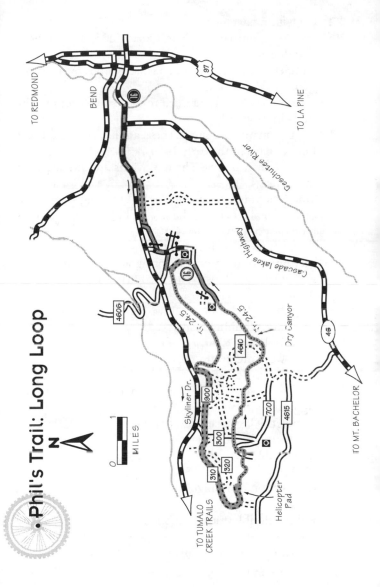

Phil's Trail: Long Loop

N

0 ___ 1
MILES

TO REDMOND

BEND

16

97

TO LA PINE

Deschutes River

Cascade Lakes Highway

46

TO MT. BACHELOR

4606

Skyliner Dr.

16

Tr. 24.5

Tr. 24.5

4610

Dry Canyon

900

300

310

320

700

4615

Helicopter Pad

TO TUMALO CREEK TRAILS

71

3.2 Go left on pavement.

3.6 Turn right onto gravel Forest Road 4606, marked with a trailhead sign.

3.8 Turn left onto a trail that immediately hops over a small berm.

4.0 A trail goes left (the return route); stay straight. The trail climbs gently.

5.3 First of many can piles. These are left over from the lumber days of the early 1900s.

5.4 Enter a burned area. The trail winds around and over many snags.

5.8 Trail junction. Go right and begin climbing steeply out of this small ravine. (The left trail is part of the short loop described in Ride 17.)

6.7 Turn left onto FR 4610, away from Skyliner Road. This section of doubletrack climbs gradually and is often very dusty and loose. The tread firms up again within 0.5 mile.

7.5 Doubletrack forks. Follow FR 900 to the right. Continue climbing easily.

8.0 Road forks; go right.

8.6 Four-way intersection. Go straight, continuing uphill more steeply at times.

9.2 Junction with cinder FR 300. Make a short jog to the right to continue up FR 310 on the other side.

9.35 Doubletrack goes left; go straight.

9.4 Doubletrack goes left; stay straight.

9.6 The doubletrack splits. Continue uphill to the left on FR 310.

11.0 Intersection with singletrack on left and doubletrack on right. Go straight.

11.1 Follow doubletrack to the left. This route is usually marked with a brown bike sign with a "V" for viewpoint. Climb gently toward what the locals call the "helicopter pad."

11.6 Look for a singletrack going through manzanita bushes on the right or continue on doubletrack the short distance to the top.

11.7 Roll onto the helicopter pad at top of the hill marked with whitewashed rocks. Now get ready for a highly technical downhill section.

11.8 Singletrack drops through boulder field. Use extreme caution if attempting this masochistic joyride. The route continues to descend steeply for the next 0.5 mile, minus the boulders.

12.3 Trail intersects doubletrack at bottom of the hill. Continue left, which some would consider to be straight.

12.4 Cross doubletrack and begin riding on singletrack again.

12.5 Descend steeply with a couple of switchbacks thrown in to keep you honest.

12.9 Cross doubletrack. The trail jogs slightly to the left.

13.3 Cross cinder FR 300. The grade eases up considerably for most of the remaining downhill—let gravity takes its course as the trail drops through second-growth pine forest. Don't let your teeth dry out from grinning so much.

14.3 Cross doubletrack.

14.8 Trail junction. Go right to complete the loop. Begin an series of nicely banked corners with one that's a little tighter than the rest.

15.5 Intersect dirt FR 4010. Continue on the singletrack, which drops more steeply and technically through an interesting dry canyon.

17.1 The trail follows an old doubletrack as it comes out of the canyon.

17.4 Now roll onto a white cinder road, which comes from the pumice pit on the left.

17.7 Closed road goes left. Continue down the cinder road to the right.

18.0 Look for a brown bike sign on the left, as the trail leaves the wide cinder road and begins following an old doubletrack.

18.3 The trail goes left down a short descent. Carry some speed for the climb on the other side, which is both steeper and longer.

18.7 Go right as the trail joins the uphill portion of this loop. Ride down to FR 4606.

18.9 Head right on the wide cinder route of FR 4606.

19.1 Intersect unmarked paved road. If you parked here your ride is done. If not, follow the same route back to town.

22.8 Back at Galveston Street bridge.

Phil's Trail: Short Loop

Location: Just west of Bend in the Cascade foothills.

Distance: 15.1-mile loop.

Time: 1.5 to 3 hours.

Elevation gain: 950 feet.

Tread: 6.8 miles on singletrack; 4.2 miles on doubletrack; 1.9 miles on gravel road; 2.2 miles on pavement.

Season: Spring, summer, fall.

Aerobic level: Moderate. Most of the climbing is gradual.

Technical difficulty: 2+. The only technical section is through the dry canyon.

Hazards: Loose tread, rocky section through dry canyon. Numerous old doubletracks intersect the route (watch for brown bike signs to stay on course). In general, these side tracks are mentioned in the text only when the correct route is unclear.

Highlights: Incredible singletrack cruising through the forest, occasional views, lots of wildlife.

Land status: Deschutes National Forest, Bend District.

Maps: Mountain Biking Central Oregon.

Access: Ride this loop from Bend, starting at the Galveston Street bridge over the Deschutes River. To drive the 3 miles to the trailhead, follow the ride description to mile 3.8.

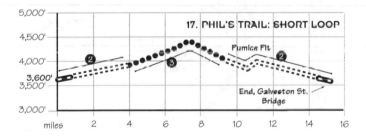

The ride:

0.0   From the Galveston Street bridge go west up Galveston, which becomes Skyliner Road after a four-way stop.

0.7   Just after a pumice pit on the left, drop onto double-track that parallels Skyliner Road.

2.4   Powerline doubletrack goes left; stay straight.

75

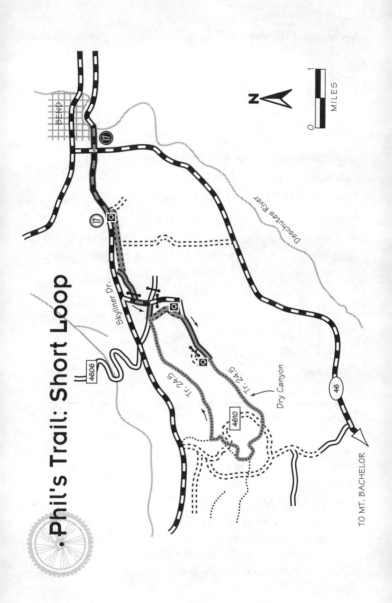

Phil's Trail: Short Loop

BEND

17

17

4606

Skyliner Dr.

Tr: 24.5

Tr: 24.5

Dry Canyon

4610

Deschutes River

46

TO MT. BACHELOR

N

0   1
MILES

76

2.8   Follow a gravel road going left (not doubletrack).

3.2   Go left on pavement.

3.6   Turn right onto gravel Forest Road 4606, marked with a trailhead sign.

3.8   Turn left onto the trail, rolling over a small berm.

4.0   A trail goes left (it's the return leg); stay straight and begin a gentle climb.

5.3   First of many can piles. These are left over from the lumber days of the early 1900s.

5.4   Enter a burned area. The trail winds around and over many snags

5.8   Trail junction. Go left on singletrack, out of the burned area and back into the forest. (Going right here continues the long loop described in Ride 16).

5.9   The trail splits at the bottom of a steep hill. Go either way—both routes offer tough climbing, but going left is slightly easier.

6.0   Trails rejoin. Continue climbing steeply.

6.3   Cross dirt FR 4610. Continue climbing.

6.6   Singletrack intersection after a short descent. Go left, uphill.

7.1   Junction with singletrack. Keep left as the trail descends gently through a fun section of banked turns. (The trail coming in from the left is the continuance of the long loop described in Ride 16).

7.8   Cross dirt FR 4610 and continue on singletrack. The trail drops more steeply and technically through an interesting dry canyon.

9.4   The trail switches to old doubletrack as it comes out of the canyon.

9.7   Now roll onto a white cinder road, which comes from the pumice pit on the left.

10.0 A closed road goes left; continue down the cinder road to the right.

10.3 Look for a brown bike sign on the left and crank onto an old doubletrack.

10.6 The trail goes left down a short descent—carry some speed for the steeper and longer climb up the other side.

11.0 The trail joins the uphill portion of this loop. Go right and ride down to FR 4606.

11.2 Head right on the wide cinder route of FR 4606.

11.4 Intersect an unmarked paved road. If you parked here, your ride is done. All others follow the same route back to town.

15.1 Roll up to the Galveston Street bridge.

Deschutes River Trail

Location: Along the Deschutes River between Bend and Sunriver.

Distance: A 30-mile round trip to Benham Falls from Bend, or a 20.8-mile round trip from Tournament Lane in Sunriver to Meadow Camp.

Time: 1.5 to 3 hours one way.

Elevation gain: 975 feet one way from Bend, or 1,475 feet round-trip.

Tread: From Bend: 17.6 miles on singletrack; 7.6 miles on gravel road; 4.8 miles on pavement. From Sunriver: 17.6 miles on singletrack; 3.2 miles on doubletrack.

Season: Year-round, snowpack permitting. The lower leg near Bend typically sees much less snow, while the leg closer to Sunriver is usually snow covered in winter.

Aerobic level: Easy to moderate.

Technical difficulty: 2+.

Hazards: Mosquitoes and hikers and bikers can be heavy in summer. Please use extra caution and courtesy on this popular trail.

Highlights: Beautiful scenery, including three class 5 falls on the Deschutes River and lava flows; rolling singletrack.

Land status: Deschutes National Forest, Bend District.

Maps: Mountain Biking Central Oregon.

Access: For a long ride pedal this one from Bend, starting at the Galveston Street bridge over the Deschutes River. Or drive to the trailhead 6.2 miles up the Cascade Lakes Highway (Oregon Highway 46) at the Meadow Picnic Area.

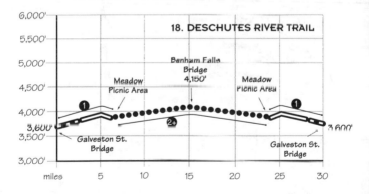

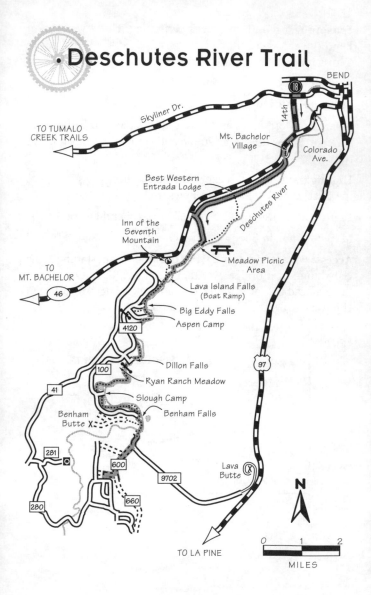

Deschutes River Trail

BEND

Skyliner Dr.

TO TUMALO
CREEK TRAILS

14th

Mt. Bachelor
Village

Colorado
Ave.

Best Western
Entrada Lodge

Deschutes River

Inn of the
Seventh
Mountain

Meadow Picnic
Area

TO
MT. BACHELOR

46

Lava Island Falls
(Boat Ramp)

Big Eddy Falls

Aspen Camp

4120

97

Dillon Falls

100

Ryan Ranch Meadow

41

Slough Camp

Benham
Butte

Benham Falls

281

600

Lava
Butte

9702

280

660

N

0   1   2
MILES

TO LA PINE

The ride:

0.0   From the Galveston Street bridge, pedal west up Galveston to 14th Street at the four-way stop and go left. Continue west on OR 46.

2.4   At the west entrance to Bachelor Village, turn west onto the cinder road that parallels OR 46 on the south side.

3.6   Go through the Best Western Entrada Lodge parking lot to continue up the cinder road paralleling the highway. (The singletrack going up the hill to the left passes through sensitive deer wintering grounds. The USDA Forest Service asks bikers to avoid this trail.)

5.0   Turn left onto a cinder road to the Meadow Picnic Area.

6.2   Roll into the Meadow Picnic Area and pick up singletrack at the upriver end of the gravel road. The trail climbs a sidehill above the river.

6.7   Trail junction. Go left above a pond (the trail going right leads to the Inn of the Seventh Mountain).

7.5   Lava Island Boat Ramp. Follow singletrack on the far side of the parking lot as it rolls along the riverbank.

8.3   Trail skims a dirt road.

8.5   Big Eddy Rapids. Look for rafters and hikers along this stretch.

8.6   Parking for Big Eddy Rapids. Follow the singletrack going left.

9.7   Aspen Camp. Follow the trail on the far side of the parking lot.

10.2 A hiker trail goes left. Stay right and begin climbing steeply away from the river.

10.3 The trail skirts a road, then winds through some tight lava formations.

10.7 Hiker trail goes left; stay right.

10.9 Dillon Falls. Check out the cataract below from many lofty vantage points.

11.0 Dillon Falls Campground. The trail follows the gravel access road briefly.

11.2 Trail starts again and passes through a gate at north end of Ryan Ranch Meadow.

11.5 Trail passes through gate at the south end of Ryan Ranch Meadow and heads back into the trees.

12.9 Slough Camp. Pick up trail again on the far side of the parking lot.

13.2 After a series of whoop-dee-doos, begin climbing above the river.

14.0 The trail splits. Climb steeply, either left or straight.

14.2 The trails rejoin.

14.4 Parking area at Benham Falls. The overlook is worth a visit. Then go up the hill to the parking area and continue left along the river.

14.7 A steep trail climbs away to the right; stay straight. (This trail leads to the top of Benham Butte.)

15.0 Footbridge over the Deschutes River. Turn around and retrace your route back to Bend at this point.

30.0 Return to the Galveston Street bridge in Bend.

For riders coming from Sunriver:

0.0 Start across from the north end of Tournament Lane Loop. Follow doubletrack north.

0.2 Intersection; follow doubletrack right.

0.3 Intersection; follow doubletrack left.

0.9 Intersection; go straight.

1.1 Intersection; follow less-defined doubletrack left.

1.4 Go left on a cinder road to the bottom of the hill.

1.6 Go over berm at the corner and run downhill on singletrack to a footbridge over the Deschutes River. From here, ride the Deschutes River Trail to mile 6.2 in the ride description above and return to Sunriver by retracing your tracks.

Inn Loop

Location: In the Cascades foothills west of Bend.

Distance: 12-mile loop.

Time: 1 to 2 hours.

Elevation gain: 1,000 feet.

Tread: 2 miles on gravel road; 0.6 mile on paved road; 9.4 miles on doubletrack.

Season: Spring, summer, fall.

Aerobic level: Moderate.

Technical difficulty: 2, with some loose tread.

Hazards: Loose soil during midsummer, many intersecting doubletracks.

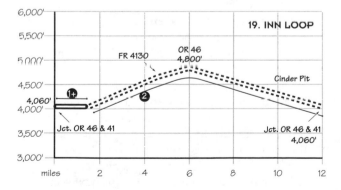

Highlights: Fast doubletrack descent, views from quarry site, route is well signed.

Land status: Deschutes National Forest, Bend District.

Maps: Mountain Biking Central Oregon.

Access: From Bend drive or pedal 6 miles west on the Cascade Lakes Highway (Oregon Highway 46) to the junction with Forest Road 41. Park well off the side of the road on FR 41.

The ride:

0.0   Pedal south along gravel FR 41.

1.3   Take a soft right onto doubletrack Forest Road 4110. Begin climbing gradually.

1.5   Doubletrack goes left; stay straight. This ride is intersected by many doubletrack roads, some faint, others well defined. To stay on the right course, follow the brown route signs and read this text and accompanying maps closely.

1.6   The road splits. Go left, uphill.

2.2   Doubletrack goes right; stay straight.

2.5   Doubletrack goes left; continue straight.

2.6   FR 600 goes left; stay straight.

2.8   Doubletrack goes right; keep straight.

3.1   Cross the powerline road and continue straight.

4.6   Turn right onto FR 4130 and find a climbing rhythm for the next 1.3 miles.

5.1   Cross the powerline road and continue straight.

5.9   Turn right onto gravel FR 4613 to paved OR 46. (Going left at this point accesses the Kiwa Butte Loop, described in Ride 20.)

6.0   Turn right onto OR 46 and zip downhill.

6.3   Turn left on FR 4612, then make a quick right onto FR 200. For aspiring downhill racers this next section is a

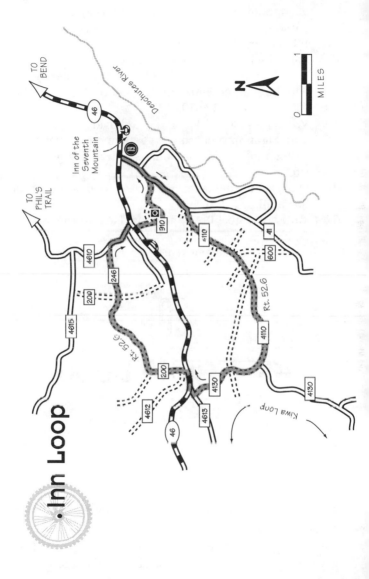

· Inn Loop

TO BEND

TO PHIL'S TRAIL

Deschutes River

Inn of the Seventh Mountain

Rt. 52.6

Kiwa Loop

46

4610

4615

200

246

310

4110

41

600

4110

4130

4130

4150

4613

4612

200

46

N

MILES

0   1

good training run with fast straight-aways, some tight
corners, and a few jumps thrown in for good measure.

7.0   FR 220 goes left; stay right.

7.9   Faint doubletrack; stay straight.

8.2   Cross doubletrack. The lip of this road creates a jump
      with huge air potential if you're not ready.

9.6   Go right onto FR 4610.

9.9   Veer left as FR 4610 joins a gravel road.

10.2 Turn right onto paved OR 46, then cross over to FR
      910, doubletrack that climbs south to a large quarry
      site.

10.8 Quarry site. After taking in the view, head northeast and
      downhill on FR 910.

11.4 Turn left onto FR 41 and pedal back to the starting
      point.

12.0 Close the loop at your vehicle where FR 41 joins OR 46.

Kiwa Butte Loop

Location: The Cascades foothills west of Bend.

Distance: 10-mile loop.

Time: 1 to 2 hours.

Elevation gain: 1,000 feet.

Tread: 2 miles on gravel road; 8 miles on doubletrack.

Season: Late spring, summer, and fall. As with many trails in
central Oregon, the riding on this loop is best after a good rain
or early in the season before the soil has dried out too much.

Aerobic level: Moderate.

Technical difficulty: 2+, with some loose tread.

Hazards: Loose soil during midsummer, many intersecting doubletracks.

Highlights: Fast doubletrack, views from Kiwa Butte, wildlife sightings, lightly used route.

Land status: Deschutes National Forest, Bend District.

Maps: Mountain Biking Central Oregon.

Access: From Bend drive 10 miles west on the Cascade Lakes Highway (Oregon Highway 46). Turn left onto gravel Forest Road 4613 and park on the shoulder of the road.

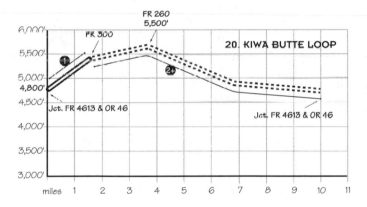

•Kiwa Butte Loop

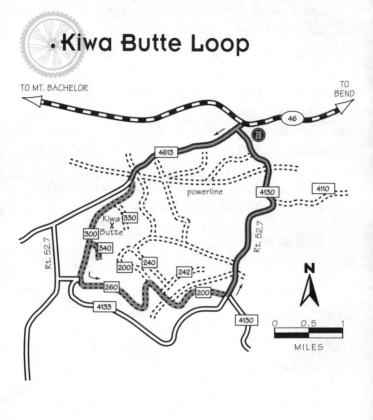

TO MT. BACHELOR

TO BEND

46

20

4613

powerline

4130

4110

Kiwa X Butte

330

300

340

Rt. 52.7

200

240

242

200

260

4133

4130

Rt. 52.7

N

0   0.5   1

MILES

The ride:

0.0 Pedal southwest on FR 4613, climbing steadily for 1.9 miles.

1.9 Turn left onto doubletrack FR 300, usually marked by a brown bike route sign. Many spur roads split off from FR 300—just stay on the main track. (One detour worth taking is a short climb up the spur going left at mile 3.1. This affords a great view of Mount Bachelor and Broken Top.)

3.7 Four-way intersection. Go left on FR 260, which climbs gently up the flanks of Kiwa Butte.

4.0 A clearcut here offers a nice view to the south, including the village of Sunriver and Newberry Crater. Follow the main doubletrack downhill past several spur roads. The route becomes overgrown with manzanita bushes in a few places—stay in the middle or risk losing skin to the sharp branches.

5.4 Go right onto FR 200 and enjoy 1.4 miles of rolling downhill.

6.8 Go left onto FR 4133.

6.9 Go left onto FR 4130 and stay on this doubletrack as it climbs, descends, and then climbs again to FR 4613.

10.0 Turn right onto FR 4613.

10.1. Roll down to your vehicle.

Sisters Singletrack: Short Loop

Location: 22 miles northwest of Bend, just south of the town of Sisters.

Distance: 6.6-mile loop.

Time: 30 minutes to 1.5 hours.

Elevation gain: 200 feet.

Tread: 4.5 miles on singletrack; 1.5 miles on doubletrack

Season: All year, snowpack permitting.

Aerobic level: Easy.

Technical difficulty: 2.

Hazards: Various rocky sections, some loose dirt in summer.

Highlights: Rolling singletrack, Squaw Creek Canal, wildlife. This is a good ride for beginning mountain bikers as there is little climbing and challenges are well spaced along the singletrack.

Land status: Deschutes National Forest, Sisters District.

Maps: Mountain Biking Central Oregon.

Access: From Bend drive 22 miles northwest on U.S. Highway 20. In Sisters, turn left on Three Creeks Lake Road (County Road 16) and drive two blocks south. Park at the Village Green City Park, where there is plenty of parking, fresh water, restrooms, and nice lawns for relaxing.

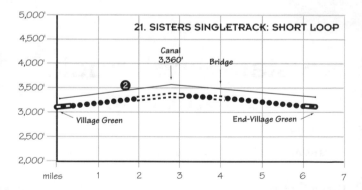

Sisters Singletrack: Short Loop

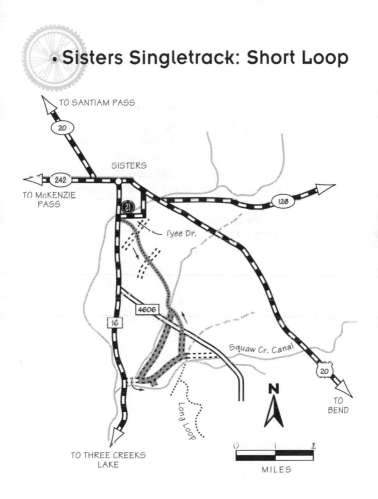

The ride:

0.0 Ride south on CR 16.

0.3 Where Tyee Drive goes left, look for the trailhead, also on the left. The singletrack crosses several doubletrack logging roads in the first couple of miles—stay on route by following brown bike signs and tire tracks.

2.0 Cross a bridge over a small irrigation ditch. The route splits just after this bridge. Go right on doubletrack (you'll come back on the singletrack). Immediately cross a gravel road and continue riding gently uphill on doubletrack.

2.8 Junction with doubletrack; go left. Look for brown bike signs marking the way.

2.9 Junction with another doubletrack; go right. Squaw Creek Canal swings in from the right.

3.1 The route leaves doubletrack and follows singletrack along Squaw Creek Canal. The burned forest here was a controlled burn conducted by the USDA Forest Service in spring 1996.

3.6 Junction with the Sisters Long Loop (see Ride 22). To complete the short loop go left on the doubletrack at this intersection. (The bridge on the right crosses Squaw Creek Canal and leads to the more difficult long loop described in Ride 22).

3.7 Junction; go right, following brown bike signs. The next section has several kelly humps that should be approached with caution or easily bypassed. Hit them with too much speed and you will do a nose wheelie and end up hosting a yard sale.

4.0 Intersection with Forest Road 4606. Cross over this gravel road and pick up the singletrack on the other side.

4.3 Return to the small bridge (same as at mile 2.0). Cross it and follow singletrack back to CR 16.

6.3   Turn right onto CR 16 and pedal back to town.

6.6   Relax on the grass at Village Green City Park.

Sisters Singletrack: Long Loop

Location: 22 miles northwest of Bend, just south of the town of Sisters.

Distance: 17-mile loop.

Time: 1.5 to 3.5 hours.

Elevation gain: 1,100 feet.

Tread: 12.5 miles on singletrack; 3.9 miles on doubletrack; 0.6 mile on pavement.

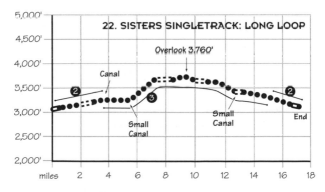

Season: Year-round, snowpack permitting.

Aerobic level: Moderate.

Technical difficulty: 3.

Hazards: Several rocky sections, some loose dirt in summer.

Highlights: Rolling singletrack; Squaw Creek Canal; incredible views of Three Sisters, Mount Jefferson, and surrounding desert.

Land status: Deschutes National Forest, Sisters District.

Maps: Mountain Biking Central Oregon.

Access: From Bend drive 22 miles northwest on U.S. Highway 20 to the town of Sisters. Turn left onto Three Creeks Lake Road (County Road 16) and drive two blocks south. Park at the Village Green City Park, where there is plenty of parking, fresh water, restrooms, and nice lawns for relaxing.

The ride:

0.0   Pedal south on CR 16.

0.3   Look for the trailhead on the left where Tyee Drive also goes left. This singletrack crosses several doubletrack logging roads in the first couple of miles. To stay on the main route, follow brown bike signs and tire tracks.

2.0   Cross a bridge over a small irrigation ditch. The route splits just after this bridge; go right on doubletrack (you'll come back on the singletrack). The doubletrack immediately crosses gravel Forest Road 4606. Look for doubletrack on the other side and begin a gentle climb.

2.8   Junction with doubletrack; go left. Look for brown route signs at this and other intersections.

2.9   Junction with another doubletrack; go right. Listen for Squaw Creek Canal on the right.

Sisters Singletrack: Long Loop

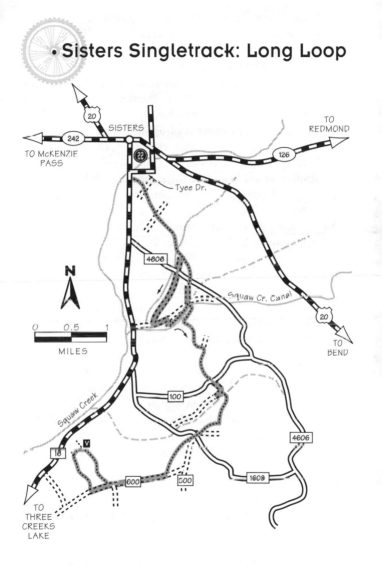

3.1 Your route leaves the doubletrack and follows singletrack along Squaw Creek Canal. The burned forest at the edge of the trail was a controlled burn conducted by the USDA Forest Service in spring 1996.

3.6 Junction with short loop (see Ride 21). To complete the long loop, cross the bridge to the right and then follow the canal upstream. (The small irrigation diversion here makes for a refreshing cool-off on the return trip.)

3.8 The trail turns left and climbs gradually toward Peterson Ridge. The desert wildflowers over this next stretch bloom from late spring through July.

5.4 Cross FR 100 and roll onto doubletrack for the next 0.2 mile.

5.6 The trail leaves the doubletrack and crosses a small irrigation canal. The passage is usually wet until mid-July. This canal also signals the beginning of the short but steep climb up Peterson Ridge. Gear down and start those deep-breathing exercises.

5.7 Begin the most technical portion of the ride, which lasts about 1 mile.

6.4 The trail crosses a gravel road and continues on the other side.

7.1 Junction with doubletrack. Veer right and out of the trees into an old burn area with outstanding views of the Three Sisters and Broken Top.

8.0 Junction with overlook loop. Go straight to ride the loop in a clockwise direction.

8.3 Go right onto singletrack and begin a series of short climbs and descents.

8.9 Watch for a brown bike sign as the route goes right on a short section of twisty singletrack.

9.1 Watch for a small dirt berm on the left at another trail junction. Go right, but not before walking out on the faint hiking trail to the ridge overlook. When you reach the edge, walk left toward some rock outcroppings for a grand view of seven snowcapped peaks, Black Butte, and the high desert. Then go right on the singletrack, which will lead back to the overlook loop junction mentioned at mile 8 above.

9.7   Overlook loop junction. Go left and follow your tracks back to the bridge over Squaw Creek Canal. The descent back to the bridge is a blast and begs for speed, but be aware of hikers and other bikers coming up the trail and be courteous.

14.1   Squaw Creek Canal. Take a break—you deserve it. To finish the ride, cross the bridge and follow the doubletrack left (instead of following the singletrack along the canal).

14.2   The road splits; veer right. Keep your eyes peeled for a series of kelly humps that should be approached with caution or bypassed (too much speed and flat landings mean much blood and pain).

14.5   Cross gravel FR 4601. Pick up the singletrack that begins on the other side.

14.7   Cross the bridge over the small irrigation canal and complete the last 2 miles of singletrack to CR 16.

16.7   Turn right onto CR 16.

17.0   Roll into Village Green City Park and kick off those sweaty shoes.

Trail 99/Road 700: Short Loop

Location: 16 miles south of Sisters on County Road 16, near Three Creeks Lake.

Distance: 11.1-mile loop.

Time: 1.5 to 2.5 hours.

Elevation gain: 1,300 feet.

Tread: 3.1 miles on singletrack; 6.5 miles on doubletrack jeep road, 0.4 mile gravel road; 0.3 mile on pavement.

Season: Midsummer through fall.

Aerobic level: Moderate to strenuous. A mix of short, steep climbs and long, steady climbs.

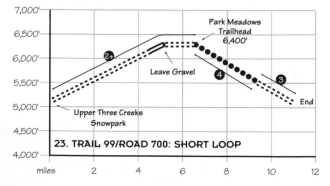

Technical difficulty: 4. Several rocky sections and drop-offs.

Hazards: The rocky sections warrant extra caution as do the first couple of miles to Park Meadows Trail, which gets heavy horse traffic.

Highlights: Pumice field, alpine meadows, a technical descent. The singletrack portion of this ride follows the Metolius-Windigo Trail, which is marked by yellow diamonds spaced about every 100 feet on trees.

Land status: Deschutes National Forest, Sisters District.

Maps: Mountain Biking Central Oregon.

Access: From Bend drive 22 miles northwest on U.S. Highway 20 to Sisters. Turn left onto Three Creeks Lake Road (County Road 16) and drive about 10 miles south. Park at the Upper Three Creeks Lake Snowpark on the left.

The ride:

0.0　From the snowpark, pedal a few hundred feet south up CR 16.

0.1　Turn right on Forest Road 700, which begins climbing immediately. Many side roads split off the route, but you must stay on FR 700 until it rejoins CR 16 near the top. The route climbs 1,100 feet during these first 5.2 miles.

3.0　Jefferson View Shelter. This cross-country ski shelter lies off the road about 20 yards on the right and affords a nice view of Mount Jefferson and Black Butte.

4.7　Road junction. Go right on CR 16, which is paved at this point but turns to gravel within a hundred yards or so.

5.2　Go right on doubletrack toward the Park Meadow Trailhead. Look for a sign denoting this route.

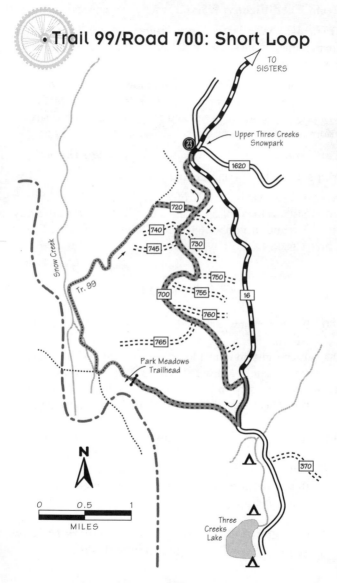

Trail 99/Road 700: Short Loop

TO SISTERS

Upper Three Creeks Snowpark

23

1620

720

740

745

730

750

700

755

16

760

765

Park Meadows Trailhead

Snow Creek

Tr. 99

N

0   0.5   1
MILES

370

Three Creeks Lake

6.0 Enter a large pumice field. (Astronauts trained in these parts before the first moon landings.)

6.4 Park Meadows Trailhead. The singletrack drops rapidly immediately after the sign. Expect rocky, technical riding over the first few miles.

7.3 Trail junction; go right. The trail descends steeply again, with one particularly technical section. (Going straight here leads into the Three Sisters Wilderness, which is closed to bikes.)

7.9 The trail briefly runs next to Snow Creek before climbing steeply away up a sidehill. Then it falls into a series of steep descents with a couple of tight switchbacks thrown in for good measure.

9.0 Cross-country ski route goes right; continue straight.

9.5 Junction with doubletrack. Go right to access FR 700 and complete the loop. (See Ride 24 for the trail continuing straight.)

9.9 Road junction; go left on FR 700. Begin the fast, technical descent back to your car.

11.0 Turn left onto CR 16.

11.1 Roll back into the Upper Three Creeks Lake Snowpark.

Trail 99/Road 700: Long Loop

Location: 16 miles south of Sisters on County Road 16, near Three Creeks Lake.

Distance: 19.5-mile loop.

Time: 2.5 to 4.5 hours.

Elevation gain: 2,600 feet.

Tread: 7.6 miles on singletrack; 6.3 miles on doubletrack jeep road; 1.8 miles on gravel road; 3.8 miles on pavement.

Season: Midsummer through fall.

Aerobic level: Strenuous, with a mix of short, steep climbs and long, steady climbs.

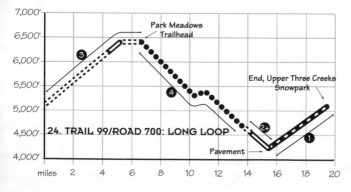

Technical difficulty: 4+. Long rocky sections, drop-offs, and tight switchbacks.

Hazards: The rocky sections warrant extra caution, as do the first couple of miles to Park Meadows Trail, which gets heavy horse traffic.

Highlights: Outstanding views, pumice field, alpine meadows, technical descent.

Land status: Deschutes National Forest, Sisters District.

Maps: Mountain Biking Central Oregon.

Access: From Bend drive 22 miles northwest on U.S. Highway 20 to Sisters. Turn left onto Three Creeks Lake Road (County Road 16) and drive about 10 miles south. Park at the Upper Three Creeks Lake Snowpark on the left.

The ride:

0.0   From the snowpark pedal a few hundred feet south up CR 16.

0.1   Turn right onto Forest Road 700, which begins climbing immediately. Many side roads split off the main route, but you must stay on FR 700 until it rejoins CR 16 near the top. The route climbs 1,100 feet during this first 5.2 miles.

3.0   Jefferson View Shelter. This cross-country ski shelter lies off the road about 20 yards on the right and affords a nice view of Mount Jefferson and Black Butte.

4.7   Road junction. Go right on CR 16, which is paved at this point but turns to gravel within 100 yards or so.

5.2   Go right on doubletrack toward the Park Meadow trailhead. Look for a sign denoting this route.

6.0   Enter a large pumice field. (Astronauts trained in these parts before the first moon landings.)

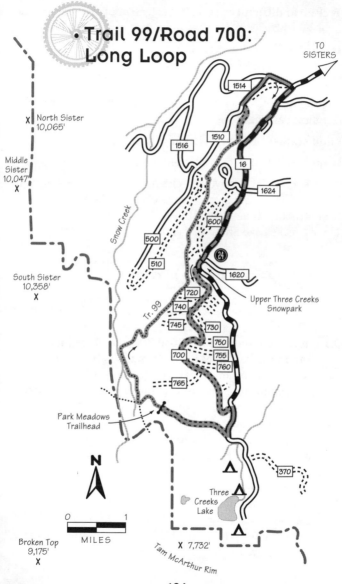

Trail 99/Road 700: Long Loop

TO SISTERS

1514

1516

1510

16

1624

600

500

510

24

1620

Upper Three Creeks Snowpark

720

740

745

730

700

750

755

760

765

Tr. 99

Snow Creek

X North Sister 10,065'

Middle Sister 10,047' X

South Sister 10,358' X

Park Meadows Trailhead

N

0 ___ 1
MILES

Broken Top 9,175' X

370

Three Creeks Lake

X 7,732'

Tam McArthur Rim

6.4 Park Meadows Trailhead. The singletrack drops rapidly immediately after the sign. Expect rocky, technical riding over the first few miles.

7.3 Trail junction; go right. The trail begins descending steeply with one particularly technical section. (Going straight here leads into the Three Sisters Wilderness, which is closed to bikes.)

7.9 The trail briefly runs next to Snow Creek before climbing steeply away up a sidehill. Then the trail falls into a series of steep descents with a couple of tight switchbacks thrown in.

9.0 Cross-country ski route goes right; continue straight.

9.5 Cross doubletrack and continue descending. (A right on this doubletrack leads back to FR 700 and the short loop; see Ride 23.)

10.3 Begin a series of short steep climbs up an exposed ridge with many spectacular viewpoints. Gear down and prepare for tough going—the trail is strewn with loose rocks and closed in tightly by manzanita bushes.

12.9 Pause for an incredible viewpoint encompassing the Cascade Range and desert lands to the north and east. Then begin the steep, technical descent off the ridge.

14.0 Singletrack ends at a clearcut. Continue descending on loose doubletrack.

14.4 Turn right onto gravel FR 1510 and schuss downhill.

15.2 Turn right onto gravel FR 1514.

15.7 Go right onto paved CR 16 and begin the long, arduous climb back up to your car.

19.5 Ugh...you made it back to the snowpark. Dig those liquid calories out of the cooler.

Burma Road Loop

Location: Gray Butte– Smith Rock area northeast of Redmond.

Distance: 11.4-mile loop.

Time: 1.5 to 3 hours.

Elevation gain: 2,400 feet.

Tread: 4.1 miles on singletrack; 7.3 miles on doubletrack.

Season: All year, snowpack permitting.

Aerobic level: Strenuous.

Technical difficulty: Mostly 3+ due to rocky sections, loose tread, and steep downhill. Climbing out of Crooked River Canyon rates a 4.

Hazards: Exposed conditions can make this ride very hot in

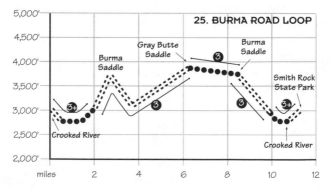

summer and cold in winter. Expect steep sidehills and stay alert for rattlesnakes.

Highlights: Incredible high desert scenery, close-up views of Smith Rock, and distant views of the Cascades.

Land status: Bureau of Land Management, Prineville District; Oregon State Parks.

Maps: Mountain Biking Central Oregon

Access: From Bend, drive 16 miles north on U.S. Highway 97 to Redmond. Continue 6 miles north on US 97 to Terrebonne and turn right onto Smith Rock Road. Drive 1 mile east and turn left onto Lambert Road at the bottom of the hill. Follow signs to Smith Rock State Park. Park in the day-use lot at Smith Rock State Park. Expect to pay a three-dollar fee.

The ride:

0.0 Before starting, look to the northeast at a road cutting steeply up the mountainside. This is the "Burma Road" and the namesake of this loop. Start by riding down the park road into Crooked River Canyon. This is the only official access to Smith Rock, and the "road" is very steep and somewhat technical.

0.5 Cross the Crooked River and go right on singletrack that hugs the river beneath 400-foot cliffs.

1.3 Begin climbing steeply out of the canyon. Portions of this section are unrideable for all but the strongest mountain bikers.

1.7 Intersect the Burma Road doubletrack. Go left and begin climbing steeply.

1.8 Cross a large irrigation canal.

2.1 Switchback. Go around a locked gate.

2.7 Roll onto the Burma Road saddle and the top of this

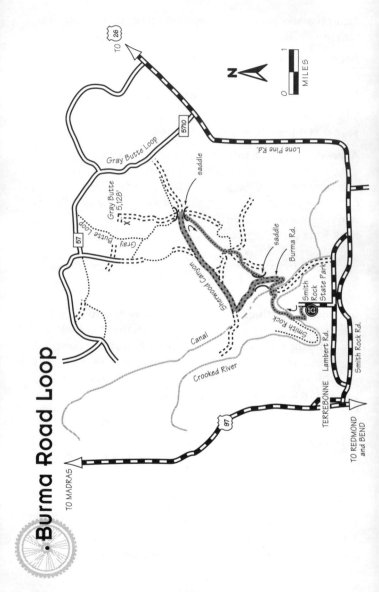

Burma Road Loop

TO MADRAS

TO 26

N

0   1
MILES

Gray Butte Loop

5710

Lone Pine Rd.

saddle

Gray Butte
5,128'
X

saddle

Gray Butte Loop

57

Burma Rd.

Sherwood Canyon

saddle

Smith Rock
State Park

Smith Rock

Canal

Lambert Rd.

Crooked River

TERREBONNE

Smith Rock Rd.

97

TO REDMOND
and BEND

climb. Enjoy the views, then continue north down the road.

3.8 Go right on doubletrack up Sherwood Canyon. (If you reach the irrigation canal again you've gone too far.)

4.8 Locked gate. Scramble over the gate and go right to continue up the canyon.

5.1 The road forks. Stay right as the route begins to climb more steeply toward another saddle.

6.3 Four-way intersection at saddle. Go right on doubletrack and look for unmarked singletrack on the right after about 50 feet. Take this singletrack, traversing a steep side slope as it rounds the hillside. Views open up to the west. (For a longer ride go left to Gray Butte; See Ride 27.)

7.3 Gate. Please close it behind you.

7.7 Four-way junction with doubletrack. Go straight and look for singletrack on the left.

8.0 The trail crosses doubletrack and continues traversing the steep hillside.

8.7 Burma Road saddle (same as mile 1.7 above). Go left and down the Burma Road. From here, follow your tracks back to Smith Rock State Park and the trailhead.

11.4 End of the loop.

Gray Butte Loop

Location: Gray Butte–Smith Rock area northeast of Redmond.

Distance: 9.2-mile loop.

Time: 1 to 2.5 hours.

Elevation gain: 1,700 feet.

Tread: 5 miles on singletrack; 4.2 miles on gravel road.

Season: All year, snowpack permitting.

Aerobic level: Moderate to strenuous.

Technical difficulty: 3, with some rocky sections and switchbacks.

Hazards: This ride can be very hot in summer and cold in winter. Watch for rattlesnakes.

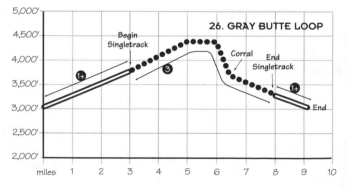

Mountain Supply
834 NW Colorado Ave.
Bend, OR 97701

No return on sale items.

Description	Qty	Price Ea	Extended
mtn biking be	1	10.95	10.95
map	1	8.95	8.95

Sub Total	19.90
Sales Tax Total	0.00
Total Amt	19.90
Paid Credit Card	19.90
Change	0.00

Credit Card   0.0000
Auth:
Amount: 19.90

_____

Customer Signature

Saturday, August 10, 2002 4:00 pm
Reg:003 Csh:r   Trns:0000051725

Highlights: Incredible desert scenery, views of distant Cascades, fun swooping singletrack, smell of desert sage after a thunderstorm.

Land status: Bureau of Land Management, Prineville District.

Maps: Mountain Biking Central Oregon.

Access: From Bend, drive 16 miles north on U.S. Highway 97 to Redmond. Continue 6 miles north on US 97 to Terrebonne and turn right onto Smith Rock Road. Drive 4 miles east and turn left on Lone Pine Road. Go another 3 miles and turn left onto gravel BLM Road 5710. Continue just over the cattle guard (about 50 yards) and park at the large pullout near the campground.

The ride:

0.0 Pedal northwest up BLM 5710. The grade is level at first but soon begins climbing.

1.0 BLM 5720 comes in on the left (you'll see it again on the return leg). Stay straight on BLM 5710 as it begins to climb more steeply.

2.3 Junction with BLM 57. Go left and continue climbing.

2.7 Begin desending

2.9 Hang a left at an old fenced-in orchard. The apples are tasty when ripe.

3.0 Look for singletrack starting at a small sign and pullout on the left. Follow this trail as it climbs gently along the flanks of Gray Butte.

3.4 Cross a rutted jeep road. Begin climbing more steeply for the next 0.5 mile.

3.9 Fenceline and gate. Please leave the gate closed after going through. The trail enters a fun rolling section and the views begin to open up toward the west.

5.1 Drop down a series of steep switchbacks—tough but rideable.

Gray Butte Loop

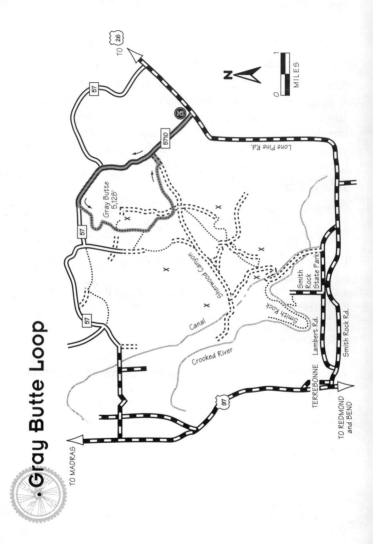

5.7 Three-way trail junction at another gate. Go left, through the gate.

6.1 Begin a series of tight corners and switchbacks as the trail descends steeply.

6.6 Trail splits. Go left over a gravel road, looking for the faint singletrack beginning again on the other side. (Diehards can grunt up the gravel road to the top of Gray Butte. This is an extremely difficult climb but quite an accomplishment if you can do it.)

6.9 Enter a corral area that is sometimes filled with cattle. Climb over the fence and scream downhill on tremendous singletrack.

8.0 The trail ends at BLM 5720. Go left and downhill toward BLM 5710.

8.2 Junction with BLM 5710. Go right to complete the ride.

9.2 Welcome back. Who brought the chips and salsa?

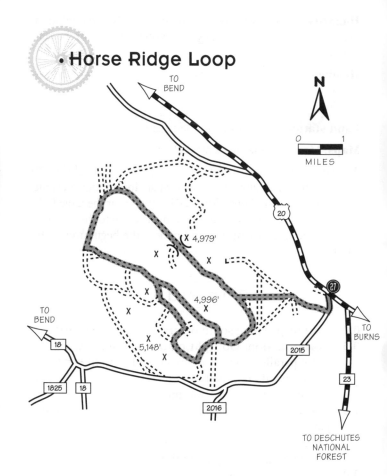

• Horse Ridge Loop

7.0 Road junction, stay left. This section of doubletrack served as the eastern fire line of a large wildfire in the summer of 1996. Notice how vegetation on the right side of the road is recovering compared to that on the left.

8.3 Four-way intersection. Go left by a corral.

8.7 Road junction. Go left and begin climbing gently toward the gap between the south and middle ridges.

9.4 Road junction. Stay straight. If your legs are itching for some technical climbing, go right and add about 1.5 miles to the loop.

10.2 The road forks; go left. The route is clearly visible, climbing straight toward a gap between the ridges. The climb ahead becomes increasingly steep near the top and is unrideable for all but the strongest cyclists.

11.5 Roll onto a saddle on the ridge. The large cement pad on the right is the top of a holding tank that provides water for grazing cattle. Begin an exciting descent toward the valley floor.

12.2 Junction with the doubletrack that circles Horse Ridge. Go left on relatively flat terrain.

14.1 Three-way junction at a cattle guard. Head right for the 2.5-mile return trip to your car.

16.6 End.

Pine Mountain Loop

Location: 26 miles east of Bend in the high desert.

Distance: 19.5-mile loop.

Time: 2 to 4 hours.

Elevation gain: 2,500 feet.

Tread: 13.5 miles on gravel road; 6 miles on doubletrack.

Season: Spring, summer, fall. This is a great ride in late spring when snow still covers the rides west of Bend.

Aerobic level: Strenuous, with lots of climbing.

Technical difficulty: 2+, with a few rocky sections and some steep downhills.

Hazards: Be prepared for wind and cold at higher elevations.

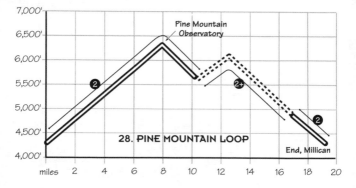

Also beware of caffeine-amped astronomers at the observatory.

Highlights: Climb from sagebrush to old-growth ponderosa forest for outstanding views from the summit.

Land status: Deschutes National Forest, Fort Rock District.

Maps: Mountain Biking Central Oregon.

Access: From Bend drive 26 miles east on U.S. Highway 20 toward Burns. Just after the Millican Store and Gas Station, turn right on the Pine Mountain Observatory access road. Park at a wide spot in the road.

The ride:

- 0.0 Pedal south on gravel Forest Road 2017 toward Pine Mountain.
- 3.0 Road junction; stay straight. Just after a small corral and trailer site, look for Forest Road 100 climbing away to the left. This is our return route.
- 5.0 Forest Road 200 goes left; continue straight.
- 5.6 FR 100 rejoins on the left; stay straight on FR 2017 as it climbs steeply through switchbacks for the next 1.5 miles.
- 6.1 Forest Road 300 goes right. Continue straight, climbing on gravel road 2017.
- 6.4 A gate blocks dirt Forest Road 350 on the right, a great side trip to a popular paragliding launch site. The main route keeps climbing on FR 2017.
- 7.0 Forest Road 400 goes right. Stay straight as the climbing eases for the last mile.
- 8.0 Pine Mountain summit. A small campground is on the right, and the Pine Mountain Observatory hunkers on the left. Ride your bike through the gate up the short climb to the large telescopes. A foot trail then finishes the climb to the true summit and a spectacular view.

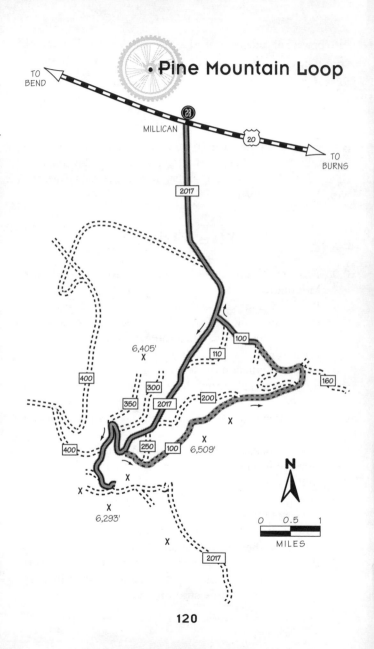

• Pine Mountain Loop

TO BEND

MILLICAN

28

20

TO BURNS

2017

100

110

6,405'
X

160

400

300

350

2017

200

250

100

X

X
6,509'

X

400

X

X
6,293'

X

N

0   0.5   1

MILES

2017

Turn around at this point and retrace your route to FR 100 (see mile 5.6 above).

10.4 Go right on FR 100. This well-graded doubletrack bends east and begins climbing moderately.

13.1 After a short downhill, FR 200 goes left. Stay straight on FR 100, dropping steadily for the next few miles.

14.1 Forest Road 170 goes left. Stay straight.

14.4 Forest roads 160 and 165 come in on the right. Stay left on FR 100 as it bends northwest.

14.9 Forest Road 140 goes left. Stay straight.

15.3 Forest Road 130 goes left. Stay straight.

16.5 Rejoin gravel FR 2017. Go right, toward Millican.

19.5 Roll up to your vehicle and dive for that cooler of frosty beverages in the back seat.

Rim Trail

Location: In Newberry National Volcanic Monument, 38 miles southeast of Bend.

Distance: 20 miles.

Time: 2.5 to 5 hours.

Elevation gain: 2,600 feet.

Tread: 17.1 miles on singletrack; 2.8 miles on gravel road; 0.1 mile on pavement.

Season: Summer and fall.

Aerobic level: Strenuous.

Technical difficulty: 3+, with long stretches of loose pumice and some rocky sections.

Hazards: Occasional horse traffic, loose pumice, some traffic on the gravel road up Paulina Peak. Plus the mountain could always erupt again.

Highlights: Views, views, views; dinner at the Paulina Lake Lodge.

Land status: Deschutes National Forest, Fort Rock District.

Maps: Mountain Biking Central Oregon.

Access: From Bend drive 23 miles southwest on U.S. Highway 97 and turn left onto Forest Road 21. Drive another 15 miles east to Paulina Lake Campground, which lies just past the guard station. The ride begins just west of the campground, where the gravel Paulina Peak access road leaves FR 21.

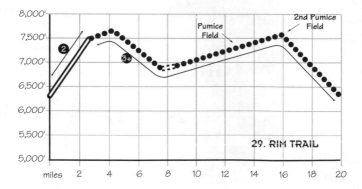

The ride:

0.0   Begin by riding south up the gravel road toward the top of Paulina Peak. This is a slow, steady climb, but the views get better as you go. Expect frequent traffic during summer and fall.

2.8   Look for a trail that crosses the road. Go right on Trail 57, down a short technical section to a junction. (Peak-baggers may opt to suffer another mile or so of climbing up the road to the summit of Paulina Peak and a view that takes in four states.)

3.1   Trail junction; go left on Trail 57. (Straight drops you off in the middle of the desert.)

4.1   Overlook. Pause here for a terrific close-up view of Paulina Peak and Paulina Lake far below.

5.4   Trail junction; stay right. (Left here heads back into the crater and down to Paulina Lake.) This marks the beginning of the loose pumice section. Watch your speed or you'll be picking the abrasive cinders out of your skin.

7.2   Trail junction; stay right again (left drops down into the crater).

7.9   Junction with a cinder doubletrack road. Head left on this road for 0.4 mile.

8.3   Junction with gravel CR 21. The singletrack begins again immediately across the road. (This is nice bailout point for those not wanting to do the whole ride — simply lean left and stay left when you hit the paved road above East Lake.)

12.7   After climbing The Wall (a short, nearly unrideable section), take a breather on the open pumice fields that slope away toward East Lake far below.

13.9   A faint trail goes left and downhill toward East Lake. Instead, stay straight.

Rim Trail

North Paulina Peak
7,686'
X

Tr. 61

Tr. 56

Resort

Tr. 57

Tr. 57

East Lake
6,381'

Paulina Lake
6,331'

7,013'
X Crater

Newberry

630

Paulina Cr.

21

TO 97

29

Obsidian Flow

Tr. 8

21

X

2127

500

Paulina Peak
7,897'
X

Tr. 57

N

0   1
MILES

15.6 Trail junction; stay left. (Trail 61, to the right, drops you far away from your car.)

16.1 Pause where the trail enters another open section of pumice for a nice view looking south toward Paulina Peak. Hold on to your pants for the next 3.7 miles of descending. Be alert for tight corners and tricky lines.

19.8 Junction with the paved road to Paulina Lake Lodge. Head left for dinner or right to get back to your car.

20.0 Anyone ready for a second lap around the crater?

Paulina Creek Trail (Peter Skene Ogden National Scenic Trail)

Location: 26 miles south of Bend in Newberry National Volcanic Monument.

Distance: 16.6 miles.

Time: 2 to 4 hours.

Elevation gain: 2,200 feet.

Tread: 8.3 miles on singletrack; 5.1 miles on doubletrack; 2.6 miles on gravel road; 0.6 mile on pavement.

Season: Summer and fall.

Aerobic level: Strenuous, with both short, steep climbs and long, steady ones.

Technical difficulty: 3+ when climbing the singletrack (several rocky sections and numerous waterbars); 2+ when descending on doubletrack and gravel roads (some loose tread and rocky sections).

Hazards: This trail is closed to downhill bike traffic due to user conflicts over the years. Please obey this restriction. This is a popular hiking and equestrian trail, so always yield the right-of-way and be courteous.

Highlights: Numerous waterfalls, views of Paulina Lake and Paulina Peak at the top of the ride, fun descent.

Land status: Deschutes National Forest, Fort Rock District.

Maps: Mountain Biking Central Oregon.

Access: From Bend drive 23 miles south on U.S. Highway 97. Turn left on the Paulina Lake access road (County Road 21) and drive about 3 miles east. Look for signs for the Ogden Group Camp on the left just before CR 21 crosses Paulina Creek. Pull in here and find the Peter Skene Ogden National Scenic Trail Trailhead on the right at a large gravel parking area with a bridge across the creek. Park here.

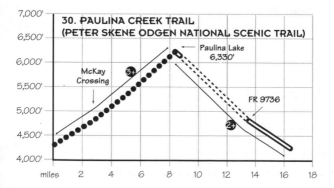

The ride:

0.0   Cross the bridge and begin climbing on singletrack.

0.7   The trail meets doubletrack. Go right and then left.

1.0   The trail crosses Paulina Creek on small footbridge. Look for the first series of waterfalls just upstream from here.

2.8   The trail crosses a gravel road at McKay Crossing Campground. The climb is fairly gradual at this point, following the grade of an old railroad bed. Loggers used the rails to haul timber out of the forest to sawmills in Bend.

3.7   The trail begins climbing more steeply. The route leaves the smooth railroad bed and becomes more technical with frequent short, steep uphills, rocky sections, and waterbars.

5.3   Trail junction. Go straight to complete entire loop or right to end climbing and shorten the loop. The trail to the right is new and crosses over the creek at a very scenic point. It continues on the other side to Forest Road 500, which is the downhill leg of this loop.

8.0   Overlook of Paulina Creek Falls. This is the largest of numerous falls on the creek.

8.3   Paulina Lake. Go right on pavement to continue the loop or left for lunch or snacks at Paulina Lake Lodge.

8.4   Junction with CR 21. Crank it downhill on pavement to the Paulina Creek Falls parking area.

8.6   Turn right into the parking area. Follow doubletrack FR 500 beneath a set of powerlines down the hill. The first section of this road can be heavily rutted and dusty; be careful.

11.2   Trail junction. This is the new access trail to the creek and uphill trail (see mile 5.3). Continue straight, down FR 500, which follows the powerlines for its entirety.

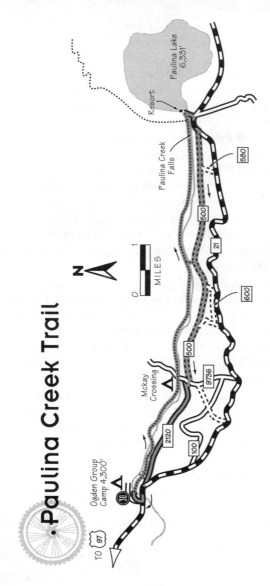

Paulina Creek Trail

Paulina Lake 6,331'

Resort

Paulina Creek Falls

580

500

21

600

N

MILES
0 1

500

9736

Mckay Crossing

500

2120

100

Ogden Group Camp 4,300'

30

TO 97

From this point on, the riding is not technical and offers some fun cruising on mainly smooth doubletrack.

11.6 The road forks. Continue right on FR 500.

13.7 Cross the gravel road that leads right to McKay Crossing Campground or left to CR 21.

13.8 Intersect gravel Road 2120. Go left as in continues dropping toward the ride's end.

16.2 Intersect paved CR 21. Go right, over Paulina Creek, and right again into Ogden Group Camp and the trailhead.

16.6 Swagger over to your car and pretend all that climbing was easy.

McKenzie River Trail

Location: On the west side of the Cascade Range, midway between Bend and Eugene.

Distance: 24.4 miles one way. A car shuttle is definitely recommended for this ride.

Time: 3 to 7 hours.

Elevation gain: 900 feet.

Tread: 23.9 miles on singletrack; 0.5 mile on gravel.

Season: Summer and fall.

Aerobic level: Moderate.

Technical difficulty: 4+ to Trail Bridge Campground; 3 for the remainder.

Hazards: This trail runs through beds of sharp lava, which is hard on tires and skin alike. In places the trail skirts sheer drops to the river far below. Be sure to take extra food and water, since this ride is much harder on the body than the bare facts indicate.

Highlights: A classic ride. This trail highlights the best of Oregon with mountain views, lush old-growth forest, an unbelievably clear river, and surprises around every corner.

Land status: Willamette National Forest, McKenzie District.

Maps: Willamette National Forest map.

Access: From Bend drive 22 miles west on U.S. Highway 20 to Sisters. Continue 26 miles west on US 20/Oregon Highway 126, over Santiam Pass, and bear left where OR 126 splits south from US 20. Drive about 2 miles south on OR 126 and look for the Old Santiam Wagon Road marker across from Fish Lake. Park at the Old Santiam Wagon Road trailhead on the east side of OR 126. The trail leaves from the south end of the parking lot. (Do not pedal down the old wagon road, which leads west down the Santiam River drainage or east through Santiam Pass and on toward Black Butte Ranch.)

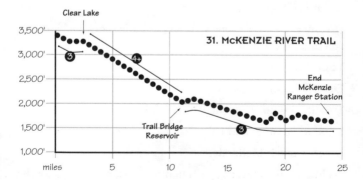

Since this is a one-way ride, arrange to have someone pick you up at the downhill end or leave a shuttle vehicle there. The McKenzie Bridge Ranger Station makes a good stopping point. It is about 24 miles south and west on OR 126 on the south side of the highway.

The ride:

0.0 The trail leaves the parking area heading due south.

0.2 Bridge over Fish Lake Creek. (Many side creeks drain into the McKenzie River, and each crossing has some form of bridge. A few are rideable, but many are too narrow to ride safely.)

0.9 The trail splits. These two forks wrap around Clear Lake and rejoin on the south end. The left fork (or east side route) traverses exposed lava flows, which make for rough riding. The right fork wanders through Clear Lake Resort and Campground. Let's go right.

1.0 West end of Clear Lake. Look beneath the surface to see an ancient forest preserved by the cold, clear water. Think twice about swimming in this lake—its temperature remains a frigid 42 degrees Fahrenheit even in the middle of summer.

1.1 Bridge over Ikenick Creek.

1.4 Resort and campground. Expect lots of campers and cars. The trail begins again along the shoreline on the far end of the campground.

2.2 Bridge over the headwaters of the McKenzie River. Soon after the crossing the bridge, the trail rejoins the east side trail. Continue south. The next 0.8 mile is technical with tight corners and sharp lava.

2.9 Cross paved Forest Road 770.

3.0 Cross OR 126. CAUTION: Watch for traffic.

3.2 Bridge over the McKenzie River.

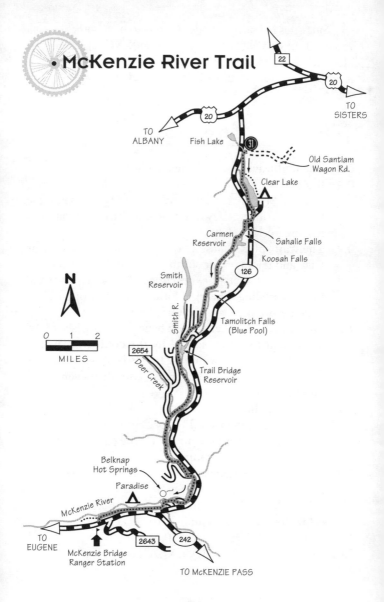

McKenzie River Trail

22

20

TO
SISTERS

20

TO
ALBANY

Fish Lake

31

Old Santiam
Wagon Rd.

Clear Lake

Carmen
Reservoir

Sahalie Falls

Koosah Falls

Smith
Reservoir

126

Smith R.

Tamolitch Falls
(Blue Pool)

2654

Trail Bridge
Reservoir

Deer Creek

Belknap
Hot Springs

Paradise

McKenzie River

TO
EUGENE

McKenzie Bridge
Ranger Station

2643

242

TO McKENZIE PASS

N

0   1   2

MILES

3.7 Sahalie Falls. Pause here to feel the power of this ice cold river as it thunders over a basalt cliff. Don't swing wide on any turns during the next section. Sheer cliffs give way to the river below

4.1 Koosah Falls. This double falls are nearly as tall as Sahalie Falls, and the mist provides welcome relief on hot summer days.

4.3 Trail junction. Left leads a short distance to Carmen Reservoir and access to OR 126. Go right to continue on the McKenzie River Trail. Impressive old-growth Douglas-fir dwarf all other lifeforms along this trail. Take the time to count the growth rings on some of the larger downed trees; a few specimens date back almost 500 years.

5.5 The trail crosses a small bridge and enters the Tamolitch Valley.

6.2 Cross another small bridge. Notice the dry riverbed here? The McKenzie River actually runs underground for a couple of miles. Except during times of unusually high runoff, no water runs above ground in this stretch.

6.5 Cross yet another small bridge. This next section to Trail Bridge Reservoir is extremely technical with many short climbs and descents through nasty lava formations.

8.0 Tamolitch Falls (Blue Pool). The McKenzie River springs up in a large pool of azure water. The only time water comes over the falls is during high runoff.

9.2 The bridge builders have been busy. Cross another.

9.7 What's this? Another bridge? You bet.

10.0 The trail crosses gravel FR 655. This is popular trailhead for hikers walking to see Tamolitch Falls.

10.6 Cross another gravel road and roll down to Trail Bridge Reservoir. Be alert for blind corners, often accompanied by steep sidehill drop-offs.

11.1 The trail drops onto a gravel road. Jog right onto the

road a short ways, then bail onto the trail again on the left. Trail Bridge Campground (across the large gravel parking area) makes a nice lunch spot.

11.2 The trail crosses a small bridge and begins climbing steeply.

11.9 The trail crosses another gravel service road (to Trail Bridge Reservoir Dam). Stay on the trail, which begins again immediately.

15.1 Cross another bridge.

15.2 Skitter across another gravel road.

16.2 Oops! A washed-out bridge. The 1996 floods wreaked havoc on many western Oregon trails, but most of the McKenzie River Trail was spared. This particular crossing was one of only two along the entire 25-mile length to sustain major damage. The USDA Forest Service will repair the bridge eventually, but riders need to pick a line over the rocks and stream to the trail, which resumes slightly downstream about 75 yards away. This crossing is very difficult (and dangerous) after heavy rains or during spring snowmelt.

17.0 The trail banks onto a gravel road. Roll south.

17.2 A washout on the road. Use care in scrambling over this usually dry creek.

17.3 Roll up to a gate and junction with a gravel road. Go through the gate and look for the trail, which begins again on the left.

18.5 Cross a bridge.

18.6 Go left on a gravel road and cross the McKenzie River (on—you guessed it—another bridge).

18.7 Junction with OR 126. The trail actually follows the highway shoulder to the right a ways before crossing a bridge and heading back into the forest.

19.4 Cross a gravel road.

19.6 Cross a gravel turnaround.

20.2 The trail joins a gravel road going right.

20.3 The trail rolls off the road on the left.

20.4 Cross a paved road (to Belknap Hot Springs).

21.2 Trail junction. Left leads back to OR 126. Stay straight.

21.8 Cross a gravel road.

22.1 Cross the bridge over Starr Creek.

22.7 A side trail going right leads to Paradise Campground. Keep straight.

22.8 Cross the paved road to Paradise Campground.

23.6 Cross a gravel road.

24.1 Look left to see a cable crossing over the river. This is used to carry supplies and people to the other side, at a much cheaper cost than constructing a bridge.

24.3 Trail junction. Go left to end the ride at McKenzie Bridge Ranger Station.

24.4 Cross OR 126 (looking both ways for traffic) and roll into the ranger station parking lot.

Appendix A
Additional Rides

Black Butte Roads to Trails

Location: 10 miles west of Sisters near Black Butte Ranch.

Distance: 10 to 20 miles, depending on route taken.

Time: 1 to 4 hours.

Elevation gain: Varies, but expect short, steep singletrack connecting relatively flat doubletrack.

Tread: 90 percent doubletrack; 10 percent singletrack.

Season: Spring, summer, fall.

Aerobic level: Moderate.

Technical difficulty: 2 on doubletrack; 3 on singletrack.

Hazards: Loose tread, manzanita bushes, tight switchbacks.

Highlights: Old-growth ponderosa forests, views of surrounding mountains, easy connections to Green Ridge or Suttle Tie trails.

Land status: Deschutes National Forest, Sisters District.

Maps: Mountain Biking Central Oregon.

Access: From Bend drive 32 miles northwest on U.S. Highway 20, passing through Sisters. About 10 miles past Sisters look for a large pullout where the Camp Sherman Road goes right. Park here. The trail system begins from the east end of the pullout.

• Black Butte Roads to Trails

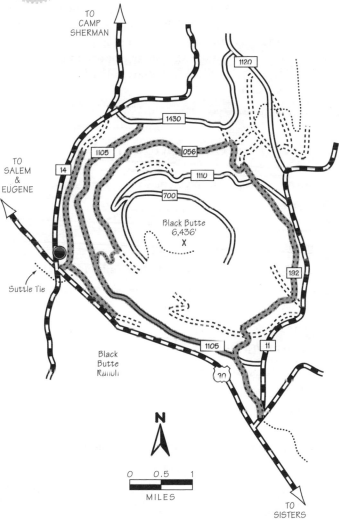

TO
CAMP
SHERMAN

1120

1430

1105   056

14   1110

700

Black Butte
6,436'
X

TO
SALEM
&
EUGENE

192

Suttle Tie

Black
Butte
Ranch

1105   11

20

N

0   0.5   1

MILES

TO
SISTERS

The ride:

The USDA Forest Service created this trail system four years ago by closing the old logging roads circling Black Butte to vehicle traffic and connecting them with singletrack. The extent of the system creates many loop options. Look at the map to come up with one to suit your tastes. In general, the higher you go, the more the trees thin out to allow views of the surrounding mountains.

Green Ridge Trail

Location: 15 miles northwest of Sisters near Camp Sherman.

Distance: 18 miles.

Time: 2 to 4 hours.

Elevation gain: 1,800 feet.

Tread: 7.2 miles on doubleback; 10.8 miles on singletrack.

Season: Late spring through fall. This ride is best done after a good rain to avoid dusty conditions.

Aerobic level: Moderate.

Technical difficulty: 2+.

Hazards: Some loose dirt and narrow tread.

Highlights: Rolling singletrack, views of Metolius River Valley and surrounding mountains. Easily connected with Black Butte Roads to Trail system.

Land status: Deschutes National Forest, Sisters District.

Maps: Mountain Biking Central Oregon.

Access: From Bend drive about 32 miles northwest on U.S.

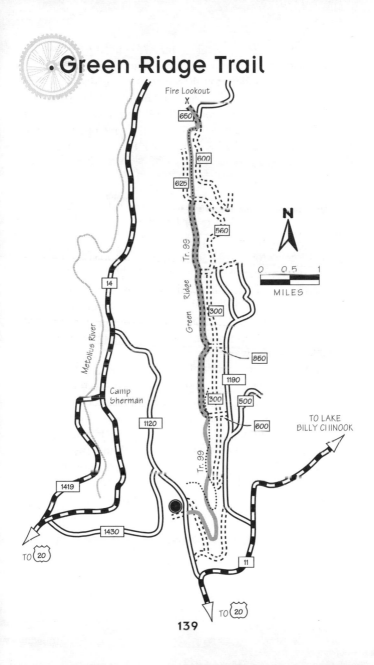

•Green Ridge Trail

Fire Lookout
X

650

600

625

560

N

0   0.5   1
MILES

Green Ridge Tr. 99

300

850

1190

300   500

600

TO LAKE
BILLY CHINOOK

14

Metolius River

Camp
Sherman

1120

Tr. 99

1419

1430

11

TO ⑳

TO ⑳

139

Highway 20, passing through Sisters. About 10 miles west of Sisters look for the Camp Sherman Road (County Road 14) going right. Follow signs toward the head of the Metolius River. When the paved road splits, go right and turn right again onto gravel Forest Road 1430. Follow FR 1430 uphill and turn right onto FR 1120. Drive about 1 mile south on FR 1120 and look for Trail 99, the Metolius–Windigo Trail. Park at the pullout on the right.

The ride:

This scenic route is not too technical but does feature a fair amount of climbing. The entire route follows the Metolius–Windigo Trail, which is marked by yellow diamonds in the trees at about 50-yard intervals. The ride described here is an out and back to the fire lookout, though shorter rides are possible by turning around earlier. Many scenic stopping points are available along the way.

From the parking area pedal across FR 1120 and spin uphill on singletrack that climbs moderately for the first few miles. The trail then joins doubletrack (Forest Road 600) running due north along Green Ridge. Veer left to stay on the Trail 99 doubletrack and ignore all the spur roads going right as you roll along the ridge. In another 3 miles the doubletrack crosses another old logging road. Continue north here, now on singletrack again. In about 1.5 miles the trail rejoins doubletrack (FR 650) for the final climb to the fire lookout atop the ridge. Return to the trailhead by retracing your tracks.

Suttle Lake Loop and Tie

Location: 10 miles northwest of Sisters near Suttle Lake.

Distance: About 12 miles.

Time: 1.5 to 3 hours.

Elevation gain: 500 feet.

Tread: 8.4 miles on singletrack; 3.6 miles on doubletrack.

Season: Late spring through fall.

Aerobic level: Easy to moderate.

Technical difficulty: 2+.

Hazards: Some loose dirt and narrow tread.

Highlights: Rolling singletrack, old-growth forest, views of Suttle Lake and Mount Washington.

Land status: Deschutes National Forest, Sisters District.

Maps: Mountain Biking Central Oregon.

Access: From Bend drive 32 miles northwest on U.S. Highway 20, passing through Sisters. About 10 miles past Sisters look for a large pullout where the Camp Sherman Road goes right. Park here. The trail starts on the south side of US 20 and is marked by a small sign.

Tho ride:

Follow the new Suttle Tie Trail as it rolls west as a firm singletrack toward Suttle Lake. The trail parallels US 20 and crosses several doubletracks on the way. Upon reaching the lake you can turn around and follow the same route back or complete the Lake Loop Trail. Expect much heavier foot traffic (as well as a few technical challenges) on the trail around the lake.

Waldo Lake Loop

Location: 55 miles southwest of Bend near Willamette Pass.

Distance: 22 miles.

Time: 3 to 8 hours.

Elevation gain: 1,500 feet.

Tread: 22 miles on singletrack.

Season: Midsummer through fall. Call first to make sure the trail has been cleared. The forest on the north side of the lake burned in August 1996. The trail itself was scorched and downfall may be abundant. Check on its status with the Oakridge Ranger District of the Willamette National Forest before heading up to the lake.

Aerobic level: Strenuous, with many short, steep climbs.

Technical difficulty: 3 on north, south, and east sides of the lake; 4+ on west side.

Hazards: Many rocky sections, roots, and waterbars. Expect swarms of mosquitoes in early and midsummer. This is a long, difficult ride with remote sections away from roads or other support. Definitely bring tools, food, and at least three water bottles.

Highlights: Incredible rolling singletrack, views across Waldo Lake to surrounding mountains. This is a "must do" trail for strong riders.

Land status: Willamette National Forest, Oakridge District.

Maps: Mountain Biking Central Oregon.

Access: From Bend drive 47 miles south on U.S. Highway 97 to the twin towns of Gilchrist and Crescent on the right. Go west on the cutoff for Oregon Highway 58 about 15 miles and continue west on OR 58 over Willamette Pass. Just over the west side of the pass turn right and drive north on the paved Waldo Lake access road (Forest Road 5897). Follow signs to Shadow Bay Campground and park near the boat ramp. Look for the trail that begins to the left of the small dock.

The ride:

Waldo Lake is among the purest in the world. With no major feeder streams and very little runoff, the water is amazingly clear—visibility can be more than 100 feet. Take some time along the way to swim or wade in the water. A couple of great locations are Klovdahl Bay, the headwaters of the North Fork Willamette River, and the North Waldo Campground swimming dock. Though the trails here are difficult in places, this ride is fun and beautiful. Clockwise is the preferred direction, though several sections are virtually unrideable in either direction. Be aware that the south, west, and north sides of the lake are bordered by the Waldo Lake Wilderness. Please do not ride off on any side trails.

Tumalo Mountain Loop

Location: 15 miles west of Bend around Tumalo Mountain.

Distance: About 18 miles.

Time: 2 to 4 hours.

Elevation gain: 1,400 feet.

Tread: 14.4 miles on singletrack; 3.6 miles on doubletrack.

Season: Midsummer through fall.

Aerobic level: Strenuous, with many short, steep climbs.

Technical difficulty: 3+.

Hazards: Root hops, tight corners, rocks.

Highlights: Incredible rolling singletrack through high alpine forest, glimpses of migrating elk herds, close-up views of mountains.

Land status: Deschutes National Forest, Bend District.

Maps: Mountain Biking Central Oregon.

Access: From Bend drive 15 miles west on Oregon Highway 46 (the Cascade Lakes Highway) to the Swampy Lakes Snowpark.

The ride:

Much of this trail was completed during summer 1996. I had the opportunity to ride most of it, but not the section from Swampy Lakes Snowpark past Dutchman Flat to the Flagline Trail. Follow the Vista Butte Trail, which goes left out of the parking area past the warming hut, until it reaches the snowmobile trail paralleling OR 46. This doubletrack leads to the Dutchman Flat Snowpark and the beginning of a new singletrack that climbs to the Flagline Trail. Turn right onto the Flagline Trail as it continues to climb the flanks of Tumalo Mountain. After climbing for a couple of miles the trail drops to the old Flagline Trail, which is now closed. Go right at this junction and proceed past the Vista Butte Tie Trail to the junction with the Swampy Lakes Trail. Head right here over a small log bridge and begin a short ascent, then a long descent back to Swampy Lakes Snowpark.

Glossary

ATB: All-terrain bicycle, a.k.a. mountain bike, sprocket rocket, fat tire flyer.

ATV: All-terrain vehicle; in this book ATV refers to motorbikes and three- and four-wheelers designed for off-road use.

Bail: Getting off the bike, usually in a hurry, and whether or not you meant to. Often a last resort.

Bunny hop: Leaping up, while riding, and lifting both wheels off the ground to jump over an obstacle (or for sheer joy).

Clean: To ride without touching a foot (or other body part) to the ground; to ride a tough section successfully.

Clipless: A type of pedal with a binding that accepts a special cleat on the soles of bike shoes. The cleat clicks in for more control and efficient pedaling, and out for safe landings (in theory).

Contour: A line on a topographic map showing a continuous elevation level over uneven ground. Also used as a verb to indicate a fairly easy or moderate grade: "The trail contours around the west flank of the mountain before the final grunt to the top."

Dab: To put a foot or hand down (or hold onto or lean on a tree or other support) while riding. If you have to dab, then you haven't ridden that piece of trail **clean.**

Downfall or Deadfall: Trees that have fallen across the trail.

Doubletrack: A trail, jeep road, ATV route, or other track with two distinct ribbons of **tread,** typically with grass growing in between. No matter which side you choose, the other rut always looks smoother.

Endo: Lifting the rear wheel off the ground and riding (or abruptly not riding) on the front wheel only. Also known, at various degrees of control and finality, as a nose wheelie, "going over the handlebars," and a face plant.

Fall line: The angle and direction of a slope; the **line** you follow when gravity is in control and you aren't.

Graded: When a gravel road is scraped level to smooth out the washboards and potholes, it has been *graded*. In this book, a road is listed as graded only if it is regularly maintained. Not all such roads are graded every year, however.

Granny gear: The lowest (easiest) gear. A combination of the smallest of the three chainrings on the bottom bracket spindle (where the pedals and crank arms attach to the bike's frame) and the largest cog on the rear cluster. Shift down to your granny gear for climbing.

Hammer: To ride hard; derived from how it feels afterward: "I'm hammered."

Hammerhead: Someone who actually enjoys feeling **hammered.** A Type-A personality rider who goes hard and fast all the time.

Kelly hump: An abrupt mound of dirt across the road or trail. These are common on old logging roads and skidder tracks, placed there to block vehicle access. At high speeds, they become launching pads for bikes and inadvertent astronauts.

Line: The route (or trajectory) between or over obstacles or through turns. **Tread** or trail refers to the ground you're riding on; the line is the path you choose within the tread (and exists mostly in the eye of the beholder).

Off-the-seat: Moving your butt behind the bike seat and over the rear tire; used for control on extremely steep descents. This position increases braking power, helps prevent **endos,** and reduces skidding.

Portage: To carry the bike, usually up a steep hill, across unrideable obstacles, or through a stream.

Quads: Thigh muscles (short for quadriceps); or maps in the USGS topographic series (short for quadrangles). Nice quads of either kind can help get you out of trouble in the backcountry.

Ratcheting: Also known as backpedaling; pedaling backwards to avoid hitting rocks or other obstacles with the pedals.

Sidehill: Where the trail crosses a slope. If the **tread** is narrow, keep your inside (uphill) pedal up to avoid hitting the ground. If the tread tilts downhill, you may have to use some body language to keep the bike plumb or vertical to avoid slipping out.

Singletrack: A trail, game run, or other track with only one ribbon of **tread.** But this is like defining an orgasm as a muscle cramp. Good singletrack is pure fun.

Spur: A side road or trail that splits off from the main route.

Surf: Riding through loose gravel or sand, when the wheels sway from side to side. Also *heavy surf:* frequent and difficult obstacles.

Suspension: A bike with front suspension has a shock-absorbing fork or stem. Rear suspension absorbs shock between the rear wheel and frame. A bike with both is said to be fully suspended.

Switchbacks: When a trail goes up a steep slope, it zigzags or *switchbacks* across the **fall line** to ease the gradient of the climb. Well-designed switchbacks make a turn with at least an 8-foot radius and remain fairly level within the turn itself. These are rare, however, and cyclists often struggle to ride through sharply angled, sloping switchbacks.

Track stand: Balancing on a bike in one place, without rolling forward appreciably. Cock the front wheel to one side and bring that pedal up to the one or two o'clock position. Now control your side-to-side balance by applying pressure on the pedals and brakes and changing the angle of the front wheel, as needed. It takes practice but really comes in handy at stoplights, on **switchbacks,** and when trying to free a foot before falling.

Tread: The riding surface, particularly regarding **singletrack.**

Water bar: A log, rock, or other barrier placed in the **tread** to divert water off the trail and prevent erosion. Peeled logs can be slippery and cause bad falls, especially when they angle sharply across the trail.

Whoop-dee-doo: A series of kelly humps used to keep vehicles off trails. Watch your speed or do the dreaded top tube tango.

A Short Index of Rides

Road Rides (includes jeep tracks and unmaintained routes)
Kiwa Butte Loop
Inn Loop
Bend Riverside Trail (not actually a road, but an extra-wide
    pathway)
Horse Ridge Loop
Pine Mountain Loop
Black Butte Roads to Trails

Sweet Singletrack Rides (may also include road and
doubletrack portions)
Phil's Trail: Long Loop
Sisters Singletrack: Long Loop
Skyliner Loop
Edison–Lava Trail
Swede Ridge Loop
Deschutes River Trail
Lemish Lake Loop
Newberry Crater
Shevlin Park Loop
Waldo Lake Loop
McKenzie River Trail

Beginner's Luck
Bend Riverside Trail
Sisters Singletrack: Short Loop
Phil's Trail: Short Loop
Deschutes River Trail
Cultus Lake Loop

Technical Tests
Edison–Lava Trail
McKenzie River Trail
Waldo Lake Loop

Bachelor Sparks Lava Loop
Charlton Lake Loop
Cache Mountain Loop
Trail 99/Road 700: Short or Long Loop

Great Climbs—the Yearn to Burn
Road 370
Pine Mountain Loop
Paulina Creek Trail
North Fork-Flagline Loop
Edison-Lava Trail
Burma Road Loop

Great Downhills
Phil's Trail: Long Loop
Gray Butte Loop
Road 370
Cache Mountain Trail
Trail 99/Road 700: Short or Long Loop

About the Author

Scott Rapp splits time between Bend and Salem, Oregon, with his wife, Amy, and dog, Henry. Together they run Pacific Crest Mountain Bike Tours, which is based in Bend. He's been riding the trails of Oregon for nine years and has been producing mountain bike maps for five years. Look for Fat Tire Publications maps in Oregon bike shops.

All books in this popular series are 6x9", regularly updated with accurate information on access, side trips, and safety.

HIKING GUIDES

Hiking Alaska
Hiking Alberta
Hiking Arizona
Hiking Arizona's Catcus Country
Hiking the Beartooths
Hiking Big Bend National Park
Hiking California
Hiking California's Desert Parks
Hiking Carlsbad Caverns &
    Guadalupe Mnts. National Parks
Hiking Colorado
Hiking the Columbia River Gorge
Hiking Florida
Hiking Georgia
Hiking Glacier &Waterton Lakes
    National Parks
Hiking Grand Canyon National Park
Hiking Great Basin National Park
Hiking Hot Springs
    in the Pacific Northwest
Hiking Idaho
Hiking Maine
Hiking Michigan
Hiking Minnesota
Hiking Montana
Hiking Nevada
Hiking New Hampshire
Hiking New Mexico
Hiking New York
Hiking North Carolina
Hiking North Cascades
Hiking Northern Arizona
Hiking Olympic National Park
Hiking Oregon

Hiking Oregon's Eagle Cap Wilderness
Hiking Oregon's Three Sisters Country
Hiking Pennsylvania
Hiking South Carolina
Hiking South Dakota's
    Black Hills Country
Hiking Southern New England
Hiking Tennessee
Hiking Texas
Hiking Utah
Hiking Utah's Summits
Hiking Vermont
Hiking Virginia
Hiking Washington
Hiking Wyoming
Hiking Wyoming's Wind River Range
Hiking Yellowstone National Park
Hiking Zion & Bryce Canyon
    National Parks
Exploring Canyonlands & Arches
    National Parks
The Trail Guide to Bob Marshall
    Country

BEST EASY DAY HIKES

Beartooths
Canyonlands & Arches
Continental Divide
Glacier & Waterton Lakes
Glen Canyon
Grand Canyon
North Cascades
Yellowstone

MORE THAN 4 MILLION COPIES SOLD!

get FALCON GUIDED

PADDLING GUIDES
Floater's Guide to Colorado
Paddling Montana
Paddling Oregon

ROCK CLIMBING GUIDES
Rock Climbing Colorado
Rock Climbing Montana
Rock Climbing New Mexico & Texas
Rock Climbing Utah

ROCKHOUNDING GUIDES
Rockhounding Arizona
Rockhound's Guide to California
Rockhound's Guide to Colorado
Rockhounding Montana
Rockhounding Nevada
Rockhound's Guide to New Mexico
Rockhounding Texas
Rockhounding Utah
Rockhounding Wyoming

BIRDING GUIDES
Birding Arizona
Birding Minnesota
Birder's Guide to Montana
Birding Texas
Birding Utah

MOUNTAIN BIKING GUIDES
Mountain Biking Arizona
Mountain Biking Colorado
Mountain Biking New Mexico
Mountain Biking New York
Mountain Biking
   Northern New England
Mountain Biking
   Southern New England
Mountain Biking Utah

LOCAL CYCLING SERIES
Bend
Boise
Bozeman
Chequamegon
Colorado Springs
Denver/Boulder
Durango
Helena
Moab

FISHING GUIDES
Fishing Alaska
Fishing Beartooths
Fishing Florida
Fishing Maine
Fishing Michigan
Fishing Montana

To order check with you local bookseller or
call FALCON® at 1-800-582-2665.
Ask for a free catalog featuring a complete list of titles.

www.falconguide.com